COMING TOGETHER

for

SPIRITUAL HEALING

COMING TOGETHER
for
SPIRITUAL HEALING

by

Douglas E. Busby, M.D., D.Min.

Copyright © 2007 by Douglas E. Busby

ISBN 0-7414-3783-X

Published by:

PUBLISHING.COM

1094 New DeHaven Street, Suite 100
West Conshohocken, PA 19428-2713
Info@buybooksontheweb.com
www.buybooksontheweb.com
Toll-free (877) BUY BOOK
Local Phone (610) 941-9999
Fax (610) 941-9959

Printed in the United States of America

Printed on Recycled Paper

Published January 2007

Dedicated to Christina, my wife and soul-mate,
for your support of my ministry.
May God's Spirit continue to empower us
for our work in spiritual healing.

Contents

Preface

My work with spiritual healing began rather late in life, after I had been a medical doctor for over 33 years, and eventually became an ordained minister. Along with many of my colleagues in both professions, I now believe that spiritual healing can play an important, if not singular, role in restoring health to body, mind, and spirit. Moreover, I have learned from personal experience that the divine energy for spiritual healing can become quite intense when we pray with strong faith and deep compassion for an ill person who genuinely desires it. So in this preface I invite you to join me on the journey that led to my writing this book on what we might say and do when we come together for spiritual healing.

My first experience with spiritual healing occurred when I was 12 years old and, in retrospect, ignited my interest in it. On the morning that my parents, little sister and I returned home to Kitchener, Ontario after vacationing "up north," I awoke with a fever, severe dizziness and, whenever I raised my head off the pillow, intense nausea and vomiting. For the trip, my parents had me lie across the back seat of the car, with a bucket near my head, and my sister sit between them. As we approached the Martyr's Shrine at Midland, Ontario, my parents expressed interest in visiting the shrine, which is dedicated to five Jesuit priests who were martyred nearby in 1649. I assured them that I would be fine staying in the car if they wished to stop there. They decided to drive into the shrine and, taking my sister along, go into the Shrine Church for just a few minutes. Moments after they left me alone, all of my symptoms suddenly disappeared. I sat up, and still feeling quite well, decided to join them in the church. Were they surprised and puzzled by my unexpected appearance! After my parents assured themselves that I had really experienced a sudden, complete recovery, they extended our visit to the shrine. We walked the beautifully landscaped Seven Stations of the Cross on the grounds of the shrine and even had a mid-morning snack in the shrine's café. One scene at the shrine made a lasting impression on me - numerous crutches, canes and braces stacked in an alcove of the church, with a sign over them saying that they had been discarded by people who had been miraculously healed while at the shrine. Years later I realized that I had also received a spiritual healing there.

In my late teens, I oscillated between choosing ministry or medicine as my future vocation. The preaching, teaching and caring of our minister at St. John's Anglican Church in Kitchener inspired me to think about ministry. Working summers in the pharmacy and x-ray departments at the Kitchener-Waterloo Hospital generated my interest in medicine. In my last year of high school, our minister contended that no one should enter ministry without first being "called" to it by God. I prayed and listened for some time for this call, and hearing nothing of the sort, decided on medicine. However, out of lingering concern for having made the right decision, I spoke about it with another minister just before I entered medical school at the University of Western Ontario in London, Ontario, in 1956. I was relieved and delighted to hear him assure me that ministry would always be an option for me, whether or not I ever heard God's call to it. So from then on, I hoped that some day I might also go to seminary to study for ministry.

As I learned neuroanatomy and physiology in medical school, two questions of profound theological significance weighed on my mind. I would, however, not find answers to them until I became involved in spiritual healing. Although I had always believed in the existence of the soul, or human spirit, "on faith," I began to wonder if it might reside in the most complex and mysterious organ of all - the brain. However, after I heard the renowned neurosurgeon, Dr. Wilder Penfield, say that he had not found any evidence of the soul there, the thought occurred to me that it might be an energy field throughout and surrounding the human body. I also began to wonder whether the human spirit can interact with our body and mind to affect our health. This question came to me during a lecture on how various physical, mental and emotional stresses can aggravate and even cause illness, as had recently been discovered by the great endocrinologist and so-called "father of stress," Dr. Hans Selye.

The world literature has blossomed with plausible answers to my questions, especially since I became engaged in healing ministry. It pictures the human spirit as an identifiable electromagnetic energy system within and around us, which I was amazed to learn was first described about 5000 years ago in the religious literature of Asia. This subtle energy system both regulates and reflects our state of health. Consequently, spiritual stress, as well as physical, mental, and emotional stresses, can disturb this system, and in turn, our health. A disturbed subtle energy system can be diagnosed and treated with various forms of complementary and alternative medicine, such as Healing Touch, Reiki, and acupuncture. Moreover, this system appears to be intimately involved in spiritual healing.

Back to my journey ...

While I was working on a graduate degree in cardiovascular biophysics in the mid-1960's, I watched televised spiritual healing by evangelists Kathryn Kuhlman and Oral Roberts with great interest. Both Kuhlman and Roberts impressed me as being charismatic personalities who used remarkably different and effective ways to uplift and attune people's spirits for calling upon God to send the Holy Spirit for healing.

Kuhlman was a dramatic preacher who began her healing services with a stream of clearly and slowly articulated theological reassurances and inspirational songs, as she walked about a large stage, raising her arms up high whenever she invoked the Holy Spirit. When she stood on stage and prayed for healing, she seemed to know who had been healed and from what illnesses, even if they were sitting far from her, such as way up in the balcony of an auditorium. As she gently touched the forehead, face or shoulders of those for whom she prayed on stage, most fell backwards and appeared to experience a moment of bliss - a phenomenon that she called "being slain in the Spirit."

Roberts was a forceful speaker who began his healing services with a gospel-based sermon that often focused on Jesus' healing miracles, as he walked forwards and backwards on a small stage, usually carrying both microphone and its stand. After an altar call, he sat on stage and prayed for those who came before him, firmly placing his right hand over an afflicted area and frequently commenting that he was feeling the power of God at work through his hand.

During Kuhlman's and Roberts' services, many people appeared to have been instantly healed, predominantly of impairing physical disorders such as paralyses, orthopedic deformities, deafness, and blindness. As I marveled at what I was observing through the lens of the television camera, I discounted trickery and began to wonder whether the power of suggestion or the Holy Spirit, or both, were responsible for this healing. Since medical research had been showing that a placebo drug, or "sugar pill," could be therapeutically effective in ill people who strongly, but mistakenly, believe that it will heal them, I presumed that the power of suggestion was operating to a certain degree in some people. I also presumed that this healing was due principally to the Holy Spirit coming in response to the prayers of Kuhlman and Roberts and their spiritually uplifted audiences, and healing as it passed through the crowd or was channeled to individuals by these apparently gifted spiritual healers.

In the 35 years that I worked full time as a medical doctor, I saw many seriously ill and injured patients who seemed to need spiritual care along with their medical care. Many times I heard them say that their illness was God's punishment for what they had done wrong. I often wondered whether guilt, anger, or despair generated by their actually believing this could interfere with healing. Many times I wanted to assure them that God does not punish us with illness, but physicians of my era in medicine simply did get involved with spiritual issues that might be affecting their patients' health.

In January of 1994, I had the opportunity to go to the Chicago Theological Seminary, as a part-time student. About that time the growing number of books and articles that were being written on the power of prayer for healing rekindled my interest in spiritual healing, so I looked forward to taking a course entitled "Healing in the New Testament." To my surprise the professor interpreted the healing "miracles" of Jesus and his apostles not as curing people of various illnesses, but as healing them in a transformative way. He noted that in Jesus' day, healthy people looked upon ill people as being out of favor with God and forced them to live at the bottom of the social ladder, despairing over their situation in life and depending on others for support. Then he said that Jesus' charismatic preaching and teaching empowered ill people to transcend the physical, mental and emotional impairments associated with their illnesses and become productive members of society. At first the professor's interpretation of Jesus' healing miracles seemed plausible to me. However, as I considered them from a medical perspective, I decided that his interpretation might pertain only to a few of them.

While in seminary, I served as the assistant minister of a church for my field experience in ministry. While there I gave my first sermon, on healing with prayer. After the service several people told me that they or someone close to them had been healed through prayer. When I mentioned to the senior minister how pleased I was to hear first hand that prayer for healing really works, he shared a remarkable personal story of spiritual healing with me. He recalled that when he was about enter the home of a young woman who was to have surgery for brain cancer the next day, he suddenly experienced an intense feeling of compassion for her and, in tears, asked God to help her. He said when he went to the hospital the following morning to visit her after surgery, he was told that it had been cancelled after pre-operative x-rays found no evidence of brain cancer.

As I drove alone to the rehearsal for my graduation from seminary in May of 1997, I began to wonder how I might best put my training and experience in ministry to use. Quite unexpectedly, I received a very clear answer from an inner voice that said to me: "You will work in healing ministry." I immediately realized that I had at last received God's call to ministry! Soon thereafter, the seminary invited me to teach a course on theology and medicine. This course included the design and conduct of a healing service, which led me to the writing of this book.

Rev. Steve Laue, Director of Spiritual Care at the La Porte Hospital in La Porte, Indiana, Sister Judian Breitenbach, Director of the Namasté Center for Holistic Education in La Porte, and my wife, Christina Dougherty, assisted in thoroughly "testing" the healing service described in this book. Rev. Dr. Rebecca Armstrong, minister, musician, and mythologist working out of Chicago, Rev. Dr. Bruce Epperly, Professor of Practical Theology at the Lancaster Theological Seminary in Lancaster, Pennsylvania, and Loretta Peters, Director of the Lindenwood Conference and Retreat Center in Donaldson, Indiana, provided many helpful comments on the book. To all of these wonderful people, I express my heartfelt gratitude.

Doug Busby

Part I

Introduction

God has given us freedom to choose how we live. We can be immoral and unethical in what we do with and to others. We can abuse ourselves with food, alcohol, tobacco and drugs, expose ourselves to toxic chemicals and infectious diseases, and place ourselves at risk for injury.

Would God punish us physically, mentally, emotionally or even spiritually for the ways that we chose to live? This question might seem foolish in light of our God-given freedom. However, it does tend to enter many people's minds, especially when they are suffering from a serious illness. How would Jesus of Nazareth answer it? I believe that Jesus would say that God does not punish us with illness, but out of unconditional love for us, desires that we be whole in body, mind and spirit.

The Gospels tell us that Jesus was a remarkable teacher, preacher and spiritual healer, and trained and commissioned his disciples for this three-part ministry. So as the early Christian Church began to form, spiritual healing continued. But within a few centuries the Church adopted the Old Testament teaching that God can punish humans for their sins by making them ill, and shifted its attention more and more from the healing of people's illnesses to the saving of their souls.

The belief that God punishes people who have sinned by striking them with illness was quite apparent in a healing service of the Church of England in 1662. The minister says to the ill person, "Wherefore, whatsoever your sickness is, know you certainly, that it is God's visitation. And for what cause soever this sickness is sent unto you; whether it be to try your patience for the example of others ... or else it be sent unto you to correct and amend in you whatsoever doth

1

offend the eyes of your heavenly Father ..." This service was used by the Episcopal Church and to some extent by other mainline churches in the United States into the early 1900's.

Currently, this sort of punishment theology is more or less implied in most mainline church services for spiritual healing. In these services we read scriptures that appear to link illness to sin (e.g., Psalm 103 says that God "forgives all your sins and heals all your diseases."). We have a prayer for the confession of sin. We use the laying of hands or anointing with oil at the same time for the forgiveness of sin as for spiritual healing. Yet we know that troublesome thoughts and emotions, stemming from the belief that illness is God's punishment for sin, can interfere with our connecting with God and each other for spiritual healing.

In this book I present a healing service that enables us to connect with God and each other for spiritual healing, with uplifted spirits and untroubled minds. I begin the book with a brief history of spiritual healing in the Judeo-Christian tradition, giving particular attention to spiritual healing by Jesus of Nazareth, to discern ways that we can connect with God and each other in a healing service. Next I describe how each of these ways of connecting shapes the design and conduct of a healing service. Finally, I provide the framework and resources for a healing service and a summary of experience with this service.

I will call the energy that comes from God for spiritual healing by various names, including: the healing energy of the Holy Spirit or God's Spirit, God's healing Spirit, God's healing energy, healing energy from God, and divine healing energy. Although the nature of this energy is unknown, the energy appears to pervade the universe. Throughout the ages what seems to be the same energy has been called by other names, such as prana, chi, ki, life-force energy, and universal energy field. However, I believe that the healing energy that we receive for spiritual healing is unique, in being intelligently directed.

I will use the term, "spiritual healing," either for the act of channeling divine healing energy or for the healing that comes from it. A spiritual healing may occur as an inner transformation, such as regaining strength and balance in body, mind and spirit in the face of suffering, adjusting to the physical and mental limitations from an illness, and coming closer to God and loved ones, especially when approaching death. Or a spiritual healing may occur as a cure or complete recovery from an illness, albeit with the possibility of some residual impairment from the illness. I believe that the healing energy of God's Spirit usually heals, but for reasons known only to God, may not cure.

The "spiritual healers" to whom I will refer have had or have the unique capacity to receive and channel divine healing energy to others. These gifted persons should not be called "faith healers," which was the term used for healing evangelists who preached that the strength of an ill person's faith in God determines whether or not that person will receive a divine healing. Although the apostle Paul stated that spiritual healing is one of the special gifts of the Spirit, he also said that those of us who are not specially gifted for spiritual healing are also capable of receiving and channeling God's healing energy. Therefore, I believe that many people who are gathered for a healing service can create powerful "common connection" with God for channeling this energy, whether or not a specially gifted spiritual healer is present.

In this book, I will quote scripture from the New International Version (NIV) of the Bible[1] with standard abbreviations for the books of the Bible. I will use inclusive language for God, except in biblical quotations. Finally, I will follow dates with B.C.E. (before Common Era) instead of B.C. (before Christ), or C.E. (Common Era) instead of A.D. (*anno domini*).

Part II

How Can We Connect for Spiritual Healing?

Spiritual Healing in Old Testament Times

The Jews of the Old Testament lived for long periods of time with the Egyptians and then Mesopotamians outside of Israel, and then with the Greeks and Romans inside of Israel. Therefore, we would assume that the Jews would have adopted at least some of the dominant beliefs, especially of the more scientifically advanced Egyptians and Greeks, as to what causes illness and how it should be treated medically and spiritually. However, when we look at these other people's beliefs about illness and compare them to those of the Jews, we find that this did not occur.

The Egyptians believed that humans beings are born healthy, but are innately susceptible to illnesses caused by many real and imaginary threats to health, including intestinal putrefaction, demons, worms, insects, and poisonous breaths as a form of witchcraft.[1,2] Priest-physicians and lay physicians were taught that no part of the body was without its own god, so like the gods they served, they tended to specialize in a particular organ or disease and refer their patients to other specialists whenever appropriate.[3] Ancient medical texts that were written on papyrus tell us that healthy people received noxious remedies to keep demons away, and ill people received purging, exorcism and a wide variety of drugs to clear the body of various disease-causing agents.[4,5]

For many centuries ill Egyptians also flocked to a temple erected over the grave of Imhotep. In life this brilliant fellow was a renowned physician, priest, architect, astronomer and advisor in the court of Pharaoh Zoser about 2980 B.C.E.[6] In death he became a medical demigod (c.2850-c.525 B.C.E.) and eventually a major deity - the Egyptian god of medicine. People who were ill would stay overnight in his temple, where they were attended by priests, who encouraged them to anticipate Imhotep's appearance to miraculously cure them.[7] Their treatment in the temple included "holy water," baths, isolation, silence, and therapeutic dreams. Later, the Greeks and then the Romans would adopt this temple care.

The societies of Mesopotamia, now largely Iraq, believed that illness was punishment for their sins by male and female gods, who allowed sinners to be attacked by various illness-causing demons swarming around them.[8,9] Consequently, the treatment of ill people by their priests, physicians, and priest-physicians included exorcism and the ingestion of noxious substances to force the demons from the body, confession followed by prayer and animal sacrifice to appease the gods, and divination, or foretelling the future or unknown by supernatural means.[10,11] Writings on ancient clay tablets tell us that Mesopotamian medicine began to transcend this supernatural approach to illness, in being able to precisely diagnose many diseases and prescribe drugs for them.[12]

The Greeks and later the Romans connected illness with fate or chance and, as the Greco-Roman literature describes, with displeasure of the gods over matters beyond human control.[13] Medicine as an art, science and profession was established in Greece by Hippocrates (c.460-c.361 B.C.E.), the so-called "father of medicine," who believed that illness was not the result of demon possession or punishment sent by the gods, but a natural process that could be treated by diet, drugs, or surgery.[14,15] We know, however, that the physicians who practiced in the Hippocratic tradition were not against calling upon the gods for help in healing! The Greeks, and to a lesser extent the Romans, erected healing temples to various gods, particularly to Asclepius, a Greek hero who was first mentioned in Homer's Iliad and later became the Greek god of medicine and healing.[16,17] As in ancient Egypt, ill people entered these temples to be served in a similar manner by priests as they slept overnight (*incubation*) on a cot (*clinic*).

Reading the Old Testament we find that the Jews had entirely different perceptions of what causes illness and how it should be treated.   These perceptions stemmed from revelations made to them by their one-and-only god, Yahweh, and their limited comprehension of the afterlife.

The Jews believed that God had absolute control over their lives, and that their ethical and moral behavior, as viewed though the eyes of God, determined whether God would provide them with good things, including health, or bad things, including illness.[18] They also believed that God 's goodness had to be experienced in this world, if at all.[19] Consequently, the Jews placed a very high value on their world and immediate rewards and punishments that came from God.

The God of the Old Testament repeatedly tells the Jews that only God has control over health and illness,[20] and will reward moral living with health and punish sinful living with illness.[21] God even says that children will be punished with illness for sins committed by their ancestors,[22] at least up to the time of the prophet Jeremiah.[23]   Several Psalms incorporate this divine reward-punishment system into them.[24]   The book of Job,[25] which is an ancient folktale possibly from Egypt or Mesopotamia,[26] stands alone in challenging this system.

The Old Testament contains many accounts of God punishing large numbers of people and individuals with illness. God struck the wandering Jews with two plagues because of their repeated unfaithfulness,[27] Miriam with leprosy[28] because she spoke out against her brother, Moses,[29] and the nation of Israel with a pestilence because David took a census of the fighting men.[30] Seemingly unfair was God's punishment of the Pharaoh and his household with great plagues because the Pharaoh took Abram's wife, Sarai, to be his own after Abram passed her off as his sister.[31] Even a prophet could be an agent for divine punishment, such as when Elisha inflicted Naaman's leprosy upon Gehazi, his servant, for lying to him.[32]

The Old Testament says little about the Jews receiving treatment from physicians, evidently for the reason that secular healing practices would be working against the will of God.[33] Moreover, numerous divinely prescribed rules,[34] apparently intended to separate the Jews from the imperfect world and so keep them holy as the children of God, were much less directed at healing the body than in purifying it.[35] The books of 2 Chronicles and Jeremiah make three references to the worthlessness of physicians.[36] In contrast, the apocryphal book of Sirach (Ecclesiasticus), written about 190 B.C.E.,[37] states that the skill of physicians and even the medicines prepared by pharmacists are gifts from God for the healing only of those who first cleanse themselves from all sin and pray to God for healing.[38]

Since Jewish physicians were instruments in the hands of God, they were held blameless following an error on their part.[39] Even when courts had to consider the possibility of negligence rather than error, they leaned towards error because of a rule stating that even though an earthly court may hold a physician innocent, God will make the final judgement.[40]

Spiritual healing is much less a feature of the Old Testament, as it is in the New Testament. Abimelech, his wife and female slaves were healed when Abraham prayed for them,[41] and King Jeroboam's withered hand was restored when an unknown prophet prayed for him.[42] The widow's dead son revived when the prophet Elijah prayed for him and laid upon him.[43] The Shunammite woman's dead son revived when Elisha responded in essentially the same way.[44] Naaman's leprosy cleared when he followed Elisha's order, given to him by a messenger, to go and wash himself seven times in the Jordan River.[45] King Hezekiah recovered from a boil after he prayed to God to heal it.[46]

Finally, the God of the Old Testament spoke through the prophets Isaiah and Malachi about coming to earth to heal.[47] And through Isaiah, God said that this healing is to come through a chosen person, a "righteous servant,"[48] who will suffer for all sin in order to heal God's flock.[49] The gospel writers, Luke and Matthew, would eventually link these prophesies to Jesus.[50]

Spiritual Healing in New Testament Times

Spiritual Healing by Jesus

In the New Testament, we discover that spiritual healing was a vital part of the ministry of Jesus, and that after his life on earth it was continued in the ministries of his followers. Nearly one-fifth of the entire Gospels describes thirty-nine separate occasions when Jesus performed spiritual healing,[51] which I have summarized and listed in Appendix A.

In discussions of spiritual healing in the New Testament, I am often asked whether the descriptions of Jesus' spiritual healing could have been misunderstood or embellished as they were passed along orally in the many years before the Gospels were written.[52] My reply has been that the first century Jews had a strong oral tradition, so we can assume that the essence of these descriptions stood the test of time.[53] However, I do point out that leprosy and demonic possession in the New Testament could have been names for different illnesses as we presently understand them.

Leprosy was not endemic in the biblical world.[54] The word, leprosy, comes from the Greek word, *lepra*, for an itchy, powdery, or scaly thickening of the skin. This word was first applied to true leprosy about 800 C.E.[55] The "leprosy" of the Gospels, and even the Old Testament, might have been one or more other skin conditions, such as psoriasis, exzema, seborrheic dermatitis, or a severe fungus infection.[56]

The belief that a demon, or evil or unclean spirit, could possess the human spirit and cause sickness was prevalent among the Jews both in Old and New Testament times,[57] albeit possession by an evil spirit is mentioned only twice in the Old Testament.[58] Nothing in the Gospels indicates that Jesus believed in demonic possession, but he might have referred to "demon" or "demons" while attempting to convince people that he had effectively dealt with what they believed was the cause of their illness.[59] Undoubtedly, various neuropsychiatric conditions occurred in the Jewish population, and could have been caused, provoked, or aggravated by belief in illness as punishment for sin, particularly if these conditions resulted in the ill person being shunned by society.[60] Moreover, we are seeing increasing credible evidence that spirits of departed persons can attach themselves to the spirits of living persons, and either cause illness or produce symptoms that mimic illness.[61] Therefore, we might hypothesize that the demon-possessed persons who are described by the gospel writers could have been suffering either from neuropsychiatric conditions or spirit attachments, or even both.[62]

The gospel accounts of Jesus' spiritual healing tell us that Jesus was deeply concerned for the health of the whole person, in restoring ill people to physical, mental, emotional, and spiritual wholeness. He approached those who were ill with compassion.[63] He knew that the causes of illness were beyond human control,[64] and refused to speculate on possible causes.[65] He so cared about people that he made every effort to heal as many who were ill with his ability to channel healing energy from God,[66] even to the point of fatigue.[67]

Jesus clearly showed that the divine healing energy is available to all people, at all times and in all places.[68] He provided spiritual healing to many persons who were off limits to Jewish piety, including ritually unclean persons such as lepers[69] and pagans.[70] He repeatedly engaged in spiritual healing on the Sabbath, even in synagogues.[71]

We find (Appendix A) that Jesus did not use any consistent technique in spiritual healing. No doubt his charisma, coupled with his commanding statements and actions, could have had the power of suggestion, leading some people to believe that they had been healed. However, Jesus performed many instantaneous cures, which could not have been due to suggestion. Moreover, he repeatedly turned attention away from himself to God's healing energy coming through him.

During spiritual healing, Jesus often used words, touch, or both, and occasionally saliva. His words for healing were usually spoken as commands. His touch for healing, as well as gospel descriptions of people being healed when they touched him, show that he was a remarkable conduit for divine healing energy. For example, after the woman with gynecologic bleeding touched his clothes and was healed, he immediately realized that power had gone out of him.[72] Use of his own saliva for healing blindness appears to reflect the prevailing Jewish belief that saliva, especially from a prominent person, can cure eye problems.[73]

Jesus' use of prayer in addition to commanding words for healing seems likely. He healed persons at a distance, as well as persons with whom he was in direct contact.[74] He told his disciples that prayer was necessary to exorcise a certain kind of demon,[75] and repeatedly assured them that whatever they asked for in prayer with faith, they would receive.[76]

We read that Jesus related faith to his spiritual healing on several occasions. He saw faith in the friends of the man who was bedridden by paralysis, before the man was healed.[77] He told the Canaanite woman that because of her faith, her daughter would be healed.[78] He told two blind men that because of their faith, their blindness would be healed.[79] He told the woman who was healed of gynecologic bleeding that her faith led to her healing.[80] He told Bartimaeus who was healed of blindness[81] and the man who returned to thank him for being healed of leprosy,[82] that their faith had made them well. After the paralysis in a centurion's servant was healed, he commented that the centurion's faith was greater than in anyone he had met in Israel.[83]

We might ask whether Jesus' use of the word, "faith," when he performed spiritual healing meant faith in his ability to perform spiritual healing or faith in God. Since Jesus was so strongly focused on awakening the people's spirits to become connected to divine energy,[84] I have no doubt that he was simply referring to faith in God.

Whenever I preach or teach about spiritual healing, or speak at a gathering for spiritual healing, I make two key statements about Jesus' healing ministry, to which many have responded with looks of surprise or gladness, and even with tears. First, I say that Jesus never asked anyone who came to him for spiritual healing what he or she, or even an ancestor, had done wrong to deserve God's punishment with illness. Second, I say that Jesus even told his disciples that he did not believe that God punishes sin with illness.[85]

But I have to be ready to explain why Jesus appeared to link sin with illness in two accounts of his spiritual healing. In first account Jesus forgave the sins of a man after healing his paralysis,[86] and in the second account he told a man to stop sinning after healing his disabling illness at the pool of Bethesda.[87] In the first account Jesus was assuring the man that forgiveness, as well as healing, comes from God.[88] In the second account Jesus recognized that the man had been malingering, or exaggerating his illness, so that he did not have to be a productive member of society.[89]

We might wonder why spiritual healing was so much a part of Jesus' ministry when Jesus was an extraordinarily charismatic teacher and preacher of the Word of God.[90] On the one hand we might presume that Jesus healed simply because he was also a remarkably gifted and compassionate spiritual healer. On the other hand we might presume that he used spiritual healing for one or more definitive purposes, such as confirming his coming as the Messiah, authenticating the gospel message, demonstrating the arrival of God's realm on earth, energizing people's faith in God, bringing people to repentance, and even establishing the Church.[91] All of these presumptions seem plausible to me, but none of them take into account the fundamental question of why God has made divine healing energy available to human beings. I believe that the answer becomes clear when we look at what Jesus embodied in all of his ministry: God's unconditional love for us, in wanting us to be whole - physically, mentally, emotionally, and spiritually.

Spiritual Healing after Jesus

The Gospels tell us that during his life, Jesus first empowered his disciples and then seventy-two others for spiritual healing,[92,93] and sent all of them to the towns and villages throughout Israel to preach and heal. The longer ending of the Gospel of Mark recounts that Jesus appeared to his disciples before his ascension and told them, "Go into all the world and preach the good news" and "those who believe: In my name they will drive out demons ... they will place their hands on sick people, and they will get well."

(16:15, 17-18) And so the spiritual healing that was very much a part of Jesus' ministry, continued.

In the book of Acts, Luke wrote that after the Pentecost the apostles and new "disciples" performed "signs and wonders" among the people,[94] indicating that possibly all of them were engaged in spiritual healing. Luke described thirteen separate occurrences of healing in their ministries, which I have summarized and listed in Appendix B.

As in Jesus' ministry, the spiritual healing that occurred within the ministries of the apostles and new disciples was usually associated with words, touch, or both. The only references made to prayer being used were when Peter raised Tabitha[95] and Paul healed Publius, the father of the chief official of Malta, of fever and dysentery.[96] In light of Jesus' teachings on the use of prayer in spiritual healing, one can assume that the other apostles and new disciples also prayed for healing. The only reference to faith was when Paul recognized the faith of the crippled man at Lystra.[97]

Unfortunately, Jesus' ministry did not erase the Old Testament belief in illness as God's punishment for sin, as we read in Acts, Paul's letters to the Corinthians, and the anonymous letter to the Hebrews. Ananias and then his wife Sapphira suddenly died when confronted by Peter for lying about sharing all of their possessions with the others in the Early Church.[98] The Jewish sorcerer Bar-Jesus (Elymas), who was opposed to teaching about Jesus Christ, became blind as Paul predicted.[99] Paul wrote to the Corinthians that the reason for many of them being weak and sick was the unworthy manner in which they had participated in the Lord's Supper.[100] He also said that God has sent him an affliction ("thorn") of some sort to keep him humble.[101] The letter to the Hebrews reiterates the Old Testament proverb[102] "My son, do not make light of the Lord's discipline, and do not lose heart when he rebukes you, because God disciplines those he loves, and punishes everyone he accepts as a son."[103]

Paul wrote to the early Church at Corinth that certain people are uniquely capable of performing spiritual healing as a special gift from God.[104] He stated that: "To one there is given through the Spirit the message of wisdom ... to another gifts of healing by that one Spirit."[105] However, he also wrote that everyone has God's gift for spiritual healing, albeit the capacity to use this gift is much greater in some people than in others. He said, "There are different kinds of gifts, but the same Spirit. There are different kinds of service, but the same Lord. There are different kinds of working, but the same God works all of them in all men."[106]

In the letter of James, the historical record of spiritual healing in the New Testament closes with instructions on how spiritual healing was conducted. As I will describe in the next section, a subsequent mistranslation of these instructions did serious harm to the practice of spiritual healing within the Western Church for many centuries. James wrote, "Is any of you sick? He should call the elders of the church to pray over him and anoint him with oil in the name of the Lord. And the prayer offered in faith will make the sick person well; the Lord will raise him up. If he has sinned, he will be forgiven. Therefore confess your sins to each other and pray for each other so that you may be healed. The prayer of a righteous man is powerful and effective." (5:14-16)

These instructions in James' letter tell us that spiritual healing was being performed principally if not entirely by the elders, or leaders, of Christian communities, rather than simply by gatherings of Christians. We can presume from what Paul said about some people having the capability to perform spiritual healing as a gift through the Holy Spirit, that at least some and perhaps all of the leaders to whom James was referring possessed this gift. The leaders would come and pray for the healing of an ill person and anoint that person with oil (unction), as Jesus' disciples had done.[107] They prayed in Jesus' name, as Jesus had directed.[108] "In my name" in Aramaic, the language that Jesus spoke, means in essence, "as I would do it."[109]

James' instructions regarding spiritual healing may seem to link illness to God's punishment for sin. However, I believe that they do not do so, for two reasons. First, James does not say that confession of sin to God is required before or during prayer for the healing of an illness, in order for God to turn divine punishment into reward and heal the repentant. Rather, he says that the God will heal the ill person, and if that person has sinned, will also forgive her or him. Second, James says that sins are to be confessed to each other, which heals relationships, and in turn fosters compassion and prayer as key factors in connecting to God and to each other for spiritual healing.

Spiritual Healing from Biblical Times to the Present

From the writings of the Early Church we learn that spiritual healing remained very much a part of its ministry as Christians shared their conviction that their God was both a loving and healing God.[110] Deacons were designated to serve those who were ill and to give their names to the bishop who would pray for them.[111] Numerous spiritual healing events were described by such great theologians as Justin Martyr (c.100-c.165), Irenaeus (c.130-c.202), Tertullian (c.160-c.220), Origen (c.185-c.254), Athanasius (c.296-373), Basil the Great (c.329-379) and John Chrysostom (c.345-407).[112] We find that early spiritual healing practices included one or more of prayer, the laying on of hands, unction, exorcism, making the sign of the cross and, in time, communion as a routinely administered sacrament.[113]

In the early years of the Church, persons could enter the priesthood without being ordained simply by saying they had the distinctive "gift of the Spirit" for healing.[114] Soon, however, they had to demonstrate this special gift. Finally, all priests-to-be had to be ordained, at which time God was asked to grant the gift for spiritual healing to them.[115] Thus God's gift of spiritual healing to various individuals, as had been described by Paul, was being absorbed into the priestly office, to be sought and used through the sacraments.[116]

The practice of spiritual healing has continued to this day in the Eastern (Orthodox) Church. However, it gradually faded and eventually ceased for over 400 years in the Western (Roman Catholic) Church, stemming from Jerome's (340-420) mistranslation of "heal" in James 5:15 of the Greek Bible to "save" for the Latin (Vulgate) Bible.[117] This mistranslation appears to have been the starting point for prayer and unction increasingly being used by the Roman Catholic Church for the "saving of souls" rather than for the "healing of bodies." Notably, it has remained in the King James, Revised Standard, New Revised Standard and New Jerusalem versions of the Bible, but was corrected in the New International and Contemporary English versions of the Bible.

Evidently fueling this shift in the sacramental purpose of prayer and unction for the ill were statements made by three great theologians of the Roman Catholic Church. Augustine (354-430), Bishop of Hippo, said that sickness was sent by God to purify souls.[118] Pope Gregory the Great (540-604) said that sickness was discipline from God to bring people to repentance.[119] Thomas Aquinas (1225-1274) said that Jesus came to earth especially for the salvation of souls and that the purpose of his spiritual healing was to demonstrate divine power to people so that they could believe in his teaching.[120] Then too, Christians suffered from a series of disastrous epidemics, most especially the Black Death (bubonic and pneumonic plague) of 1347, which the incumbent pope declared was a punishment from God.[121]

Finally, the Council of Trent of the Roman Catholic Church declared in 1551 that "anointing is to be given to the sick, especially those who are in such a serious condition as to appear to have reached the end of their life. For this reason it is also called the sacrament of dying."[122] In time, this sacrament of dying would become known as "extreme unction."

In 1962, the Vatican Council II amended the declaration of the Council of Trent by adding, "Extreme unction," which may also and more properly be called 'anointing of the sick,' is not a sacrament for those only who are at the point of death. Hence, as soon as any one of the faithful begins to be in danger of death from sickness or old age, the fitting time for that person to receive this sacrament has certainly already arrived."[123] Vatican II also added, "By the sacred anointing of the sick and the prayer of the presbyters, the whole Church commends the sick to the suffering of the glorified Lord so that he may raise them up and save them (also see James 5:14-15)."[124] In spite of these additions, the Roman Catholic Church apparently has still not accepted the fact of Jerome's mistranslation of "heal" to "save."

Prior to the thirteenth century, physicians worked with priests in attending to the physical, mental, emotional, and spiritual needs of the ill, and priests could even practice medicine until banned from doing so by the Council of Tours in 1163.[125] Unfortunately, the religious philosophy espoused by Thomas Aquinas challenged this holistic approach to caring for the ill.

Aquinas adopted a teaching of the Greek philosopher, Aristotle, who said that humanity experiences only the natural world, whereas God exists in the realm of the supernatural and therefore can be experienced only through

the use of reason.[126]   Aquinas also believed that further
communication from God was essentially unnecessary after
Jesus' supernatural ministry.   Putting these religious
philosophies together, Aquinas wrote in his *Summa
Theologica* that any divine communication comes to us
intellectually, or through some sensory or physical medium,
so that gifts of the Spirit were no longer necessary.[127]

The Roman Catholic Church embraced Aquinas' perspective
on the supremacy of rational thought for knowing God.[128]
Then the philosopher, physicist and mathematician, René
Descartes (1596-1650), took this perspective a step further
by theorizing that our reality is made up of parallel equal
worlds of matter, including the human body, and thought,
with matter being subject to natural law and thought being
free from natural law.[129]   Descartes' theory, known as
Cartesian dualism, paved the way for the separation of
religion and science in the Enlightenment (1715-1799), an
intellectual movement in Europe that questioned traditional
beliefs, especially in religion, and emphasized the primacy of
reason and the scientific method.   And so we find that a wall
was erected between medicine and religion - a wall that has
only recently started to come down.

Luther (1483-1546) and Calvin (1509-1564), the great
Protestant reformers, echoed Aquinas in expressing their
beliefs on the reality of spiritual healing.   Luther wrote that
God dispensed the gifts of the Spirit, including healing, only
to early Christians, so that the church could do greater
works, such as teaching and converting and saving souls.[130]
However, he appears to have accepted the reality of spiritual
healing late in his life.[131]   Calvin wrote that gifts of the Spirit
were given only in the beginning to make preaching of the
Gospel wonderful.[132]

The Protestant churches in Europe and Great Britain
continued to teach that God sends illness as punishment for
sin.[133]   However, they did not adopt the Roman Catholic

sacrament of Extreme Unction. Some Protestant churches re-instituted spiritual healing, but gatherings for healing centered on confession of sin as the presumed cause of an illness, in the hope that God would be merciful and send healing.

Since the time of the Christian martyrs in the First Century, spiritual healing, often immediate, has been occurring at shrines erected to various martyrs and other "saints" of the Church and at sites of reported apparitions, particularly of Mary, the mother of Jesus. The Roman Catholic Church, which has witnessed most of this healing down through the centuries, has never formally explained it. However, Roman Catholics have always believed that in these sacred places, heavenly beings, who showed what God's grace can do in their earthly lives, help them to receive spiritual healing by praying along with them for it.

Gregory of Nyssa (c.335-c.394), brother of Basil the Great, wrote of spiritual healing at the Shrine of the Forty Martyrs, and John Chrysostom of healing at the Shrine of St. Babylas the Martyr.[134] Gregory, Bishop of Tours from 573 to 574, wrote of many being healed at the Shrine of St. Martin of Tours, and mentioned that sleeping in shrines of martyrs and saints was being practiced quite frequently.[135] Also a prominent place for healing was the Shrine of St. Willibrord, who died in 739.[136] Now we have many shrines where spiritual healing is occurring, including the Shrine of Lourdes in France, the Shrine of Fatima in Portugal, the Shrine of Knock in Ireland, and the Martyrs Shrine in Canada.

We might wonder whether the healing that occurs in Christian shrines is due to believing that spiritual healing can occur, as we see with the power of suggestion, rather than an authentic spiritual healing. In recent years, the medical profession has found that seriously ill people who have visited these shrines have experienced cures that have defied known probabilities of spontaneous remission.[137] As I have experienced, the spiritual energy in shrines where spiritual healing has been occurring is quite intense. Consequently, I firmly believe that spiritual healing, both past and present, is authentic.

Since biblical times, numerous Christians have had the special gift for spiritual healing. Most have discovered this gift while devoting their lives to caring for the sick and poor, while teaching and preaching the Word of God, or simply while having compassion for others. Historically prominent spiritual healers include Hilarion (c.291-c.371), Martin of Tours (c.330-c.397), Augustine of Canterbury (died c.604), Francis of Assisi (1181-1226), Catherine of Siena (1347-1380), Ignatius of Loyola (c.1491-1556), Francis Xavier (1506-1552), George Fox (1624-1691), and John Wesley (1703-1791).[138] In the mid-1800's, Pastor Johann Christoph Blumhart baffled the Protestant church in Germany with spiritual healing in his ministry.[139]

In the past century, many involved in the Pentecostal movement appear to have demonstrated a special gift for spiritual healing, including Kathryn Kuhlman (1907-1976),[140] William Branham (1909-1965),[141] and Oral Roberts (1918-).[142] Joel S. Goldsmith (1892-1964), a Christian mystic, and Agnes Sanford (1897-1992), an Episcopalian, discovered that they had this gift, as described in their respective best-selling books on the art of spiritual healing.[143,144] Francis MacNutt (1925-)[145] and Ron Roth (1937-)[146] first experienced this gift while serving as priests in the Roman Catholic Church.

Although some people are specially gifted for spiritual healing, I believe that anyone can connect with God for divine healing energy, not only to heal another, but also to heal oneself. Moreover, I believe that a number of people gathered for spiritual healing can create a particularly powerful common connection with God for channeling divine healing energy.

The Ways of Connecting for Spiritual Healing

The extensive history of spiritual healing in the Judeo-Christian tradition tells us that spiritual healing is an authentic, divine gift that is available to all of us when we connect with God and each other. How, then, can we make these connections when we come together for spiritual healing? Biblical accounts of spiritual healing, particularly by Jesus, and descriptions of spiritual healing since tell us that they can be made through spiritual faith, compassion, prayer and touch in the form of the laying on of hands. In Part III, I will consider how each of these ways of connecting shapes the design and conduct of a healing service.

Part III

Connecting in a Healing Service

Spiritual Faith

The apostle Paul wrote that our faith in God - what I call "spiritual faith" - is a gracious gift from God to all of us.[1] Echoing Paul's observation, we are realizing more and more that spiritual faith is an innate, or inborn, quality of the human spirit that enables us to perceive and believe that we are connected with God. What makes this possible? A few years ago Dr. Herbert Benson, a cardiologist who has written on the healing power of meditation, suggested that our chromosomes might have a "God gene" for it.[2] In his recent book, "The God Code," visionary Gregg Braden presented a fascinating case for the Hebrew name for God - Yahweh - being imprinted into our genetic structure.[3] But do we really need a physical entity, such as a gene, to generate our spiritual faith, when our spirits are already connected with God? I would think not!

Spiritual faith begins from our awareness of being connected with God or, as Einstein said, with a "superior intelligence."[4] With various experiences of God's presence in our lives, our faith is strengthened, and we become certain of our connection with God.[5]

We should distinguish spiritual faith from two other types of faith, which I will call "medical faith" and "religious faith." Both of these types of faith are associated with positive mental and emotional states that are known to have beneficial effects on preserving health and promoting healing, principally through stimulation of the body's immune system.[6] A positive mental state might include belief, trust, intent and confidence, and a positive emotional state might include optimism, hope, joy, and peace.

We have learned much about the role of medical faith in healing from the field of mind-body or psychosomatic medicine, which began to develop in the mid-1900's.[7] Medical researchers have found that strong confidence of a patient in the medical care of her or his illness, especially when coupled with an intense desire to recover from the illness, can greatly enhance the healing process.[8] They have even found that prescribing a placebo[9] can have the same healing effect when the patient strongly believes that it will be effective for his or her illness. Such findings have given rise to the new medical science of psychoneuroimmunology.

We would expect that religious faith, particularly in the form of expectant trust in God's promises, should benefit ill people much like medical faith, especially when religious faith is repeatedly reinforced through prayer and ritual. A great deal of research on religion and health has shown that religion[10] can be "good" for our physical, mental and emotional health - let alone our spiritual health.[11] In fact, various studies have found that regular participation in religious worship is associated with less hypertension, anxiety and depression, and lower risks of coronary heart disease, stroke, cancer, chronic obstructive lung disease, disability, and mortality.[12] However, as Dr. Harold Koenig, psychiatrist, has clearly pointed out, such health benefits of religion are linked more to certain health-related attributes of religion, such as discouraging high-risk behaviors, imposing dietary restrictions, and providing social support, than to religious faith *per se*.[13] Nevertheless, I believe that religious faith operates like medical faith, albeit to a degree that is not presently known.[14] Then too, spiritual faith may also be at work.

Spiritual faith differs from religious faith, in that spiritual faith stems from our spirit being connected with God, rather than from our religious beliefs and practices. Spiritual faith enables us to pray for spiritual healing with firm belief and absolute trust in God, fully confident that God will hear us and heal those for whom we pray, even if we have not experienced spiritual healing or have not witnessed it in others.[15] I believe that along with compassion, spiritual faith empowers our praying for spiritual healing and opens our spirits to receiving and channeling God's healing Spirit.

Some people who come to a healing service might be concerned that they do not have the strength of spiritual faith necessary for spiritual healing.[16] We might presume that weak faith should not prevent us from being connected with God for healing, but could prevent us from making the strongest connection possible. However, we might also presume that strength of faith either in the person who is praying or in the person who is being prayed for does not necessarily determine whether or when spiritual healing will occur: God does! Whether either or both of these presumptions are true, I believe that a healing service should begin with inspiring and reassuring "words of faith," from scripture and other resources, and in a message, all intended to strengthen spiritual faith.

As a way through which we connect with God for spiritual healing, spiritual faith should be nourished in the healing service. The service should begin with inspiring and reassuring words from scripture or other resources, and in a message. The message might include statements that spiritual faith is a gracious gift of God to all of us, and that strength of faith does not necessarily determine whether or when spiritual healing will occur.

Compassion

As I have observed and experienced so often as a physician and minister, compassion is the intense awareness of the suffering of others and a strong desire to help them. This awareness of others' suffering appears to come from empathy, or the instinctive ability to sense the emotions and feelings of others, both intellectually and emotionally. Therefore, I believe that empathy is living proof of our ability to connect with each other for spiritual healing.

Jesus had compassion throughout his ministry. He also taught its meaning in the Parable of the Lost Son.[17] This parable begins with a father dividing his estate between his two sons and ends with the father's reaction to one of the sons returning home, out of money and starving, after he squanders his half of the father's estate. Jesus said that "while he [*the son*] was still a long way off, his father saw him and was filled with compassion for him,"[18] and that the father then welcomed him home and provided for him.

Compassion is an expression of love for another person, in the way that our deeply compassionate God loves us.[19] Authentic compassion moves us into a state of caring so profound that we transcend the mental, emotional and spiritual barriers that we erect around ourselves.[20] When we rise above these barriers, we can pray for an ill person in a selfless, non-judgmental, intensely loving way. Again, I believe that compassion, along with spiritual faith, empowers our praying for spiritual healing and opens our spirits to receiving and channeling God's healing Spirit.

Compassion should be fostered in a healing service by appropriately introducing every ill person, present and not present, who desires spiritual healing. Understandably, knowing what is causing each person's suffering is conducive to creating a compassionate atmosphere. For those who do not wish to divulge this information, I believe that a few words that describe their suffering can have the same effect.

Finally, showing compassion breeds compassion. Therefore, we should give ill persons who come to a healing service as much sincere and authentic attention as is reasonable and proper, without expressing any troublesome thoughts to them.[21] This attention includes offering them physical assistance and comfort, listening attentively and sympathetically to them, and touching and embracing them if and when appropriate.

As a way through which we connect with each other and thence to God for spiritual healing, compassion should be fostered in the healing service. Every ill person who desires spiritual healing should be introduced and the nature of that person's illness divulged, as appropriate. Sincere and authentic acts of compassion lead others to feel compassion.

Prayer

Prayer for spiritual healing is simply communication with God, asking God to heal others (intercessory prayer) or ourselves (petitionary prayer). Although we create a prayer request for healing in our minds, I believe that our spirits transmit this request to God and receive God's answer in the form of intelligent healing energy. The nature of this healing energy is unknown and, in my opinion, might never be known.

The healing energy of God's Spirit should be distinguished from another type of healing energy, which I call "thought energy." This latter energy appears to promote healing when it is directed at a person who is ill.

The possible role of thought energy in healing has been of great interest to scientists for over 30 years. Numerous studies have shown that the human mind can alter the functioning of biological systems with directed thought, or intentionality.[22] This action of the mind is a telepathic, or *psi*

27

phenomenon, which quantum physicists explain using the concept of "nonlocal mind."[23] This concept is based on the assumption that everything in the universe is interconnected, thus making mind-to-mind communication for healing possible.[24] Thought energy of the nonlocal mind is believed to travel at least at the speed of light. Moreover, the intensity of this energy does not appear to decrease with distance, as do most known forms of energy, such as light and sound.[25]

Larry Dossey, physician and author, has proposed that in spiritual healing, directed thought energy of the person who prays sends a message to activate or stimulate healing in the person being prayed for, with God somehow facilitating this communication.[26] However, Dossey's premise seems to downplay God's role in spiritual healing, especially for the remarkable instantaneous healing that, in my opinion, could only come from a "supernatural" form of healing energy. Moreover, people who attend healing services often describe experiencing the presence of God's Spirit in ways that could not possibly be associated with directed thought energy. They may experience a rush of warmth or tingling passing through the body, momentary lightheadedness, and unexplained tearing. They may also hear a snapping or cracking sound like electrical static in the air. Therefore, I believe that the question of whether God facilitates directed thought energy or acts entirely on God's own for healing has no present answer.

Many books on prayer for spiritual healing provide detailed, credible descriptions of people being healed through prayer.[27] Nevertheless, the medical profession has been determined to prove scientifically whether or not God responds to intercessory prayer for healing, and so has conducted many studies on groups of people with various illnesses. I note that relatively few of these studies have been "controlled;" that is, with human subjects being randomized to prayed-for and not-prayed-for groups, and with neither the researchers nor their subjects knowing who is being prayed for.

Three major, randomized, controlled studies of the effectiveness of prayer for healing have been conducted to date. Only two of these studies, both on patients in hospital coronary care units, have yielded statistically significant data suggesting that intercessory prayer has a beneficial therapeutic effect. Below are summaries of the three studies.

The Byrd study[28]

In this study, 393 patients who were newly admitted to the coronary care unit (CCU) in the San Francisco General Hospital were randomized to receive remote, intercessory prayer (prayer group) or not (usual care group). The patients were aware that they were in this study but were not aware if they were being prayed for or not being prayed for. Their caregivers did not know to which group their patients were assigned.

First names, diagnoses and brief descriptions of prayer-group patients were given to members (intercessors) of several Protestant and Roman Catholic groups around the country. A total of five to seven intercessors prayed for an individual patient.

As compared to the usual care group, patients in the prayer group required significantly fewer diuretic medications ($p=0.05$),[29] and had significantly fewer occurrences of pneumonia ($p=0.03$), congestive heart failure ($p=0.03$), and cardiac arrest ($p=0.02$). Moreover, no patients in the prayer group and 12 patients in the usual care group required intubation ($p=0.01$).

The Harris study[30]

In this study, 990 consecutive patients who were newly admitted to the CCU at the Mid America Heart Institute in Kansas City, Missouri, were randomized to receive remote, intercessory prayer (prayer group) or not (usual care group). The patients were unaware that they were in this study. Their caregivers did not know to which group their patients were assigned.

The first names of patients in the prayer group were randomly assigned to one of 15 groups of 5 intercessors who did not know and had never met the patients and did not know others in their groups. Each intercessor had to agree with statements expressing belief in God, God's concern with individual lives, and God's responsiveness to prayers for healing on behalf of the sick. The intercessors prayed individually (not as groups), daily for 4 weeks.

CCU course scores, derived from blinded, retrospective chart review, were significantly lower for the prayer group than the usual care group ($p=0.04$). Lengths of CCU and hospital stays were not significantly different between the groups. Notably, none of the significant benefits of prayer in the Byrd study were seen in the Harris study

The Krucoff study[31]

In this study, 748 patients undergoing percutaneous coronary intervention or elective coronary catheterization in nine medical centers in the United States were randomly assigned to receive bedside music, imagery, and touch (MIT) therapy or no MIT therapy, and the sites were informed of this assignment. At the same time, the patients were randomly assigned for prayer or no prayer, but neither the sites nor the patients were informed of this assignment. Consequently, 192 patients were assigned for standard care only, 182 for prayer only, 185 for MIT therapy only, and 189 for both prayer and MIT therapy.

In the first 2 years of this study, the name, age and illness of each patient assigned for prayer were e-mailed immediately after patient randomization to each of 12 primary-tier, established Christian, Jewish, Muslim and Buddhist congregations. In the final year of the study, 12 additional congregations were added, but were not given any patient information; instead they were told to pray for the prayers in the primary-tier groups. The timing and content of prayers were defined by the routine practices of each congregation. Prayers were conducted over a period of 5 to 30 consecutive days for each patient.

The composite endpoint of major cardiovascular events, death or readmission to hospital over the 6-month period following patient randomization did not differ between prayed-for and not-prayed-for patient groups. The 6-month mortality was significantly lower in the MIT-therapy group than in the no-MIT-therapy group ($p<0.02$). The 6-month mortality was slightly but not significantly lower in patients assigned to both prayer and MIT therapy, than in those assigned standard care or prayer. Self-rated distress was significantly lower in the MIT-therapy group than in the no-MIT-therapy group ($p<0.0001$).

Failure to replicate results of the Byrd and Harris studies of intercessory prayer for healing and the consistent inability of many other studies[32] to prove what we already know from experience - that intercessory prayer brings spiritual healing - are disappointing. As a physician who been engaged in clinical research, I would say that inconsistent and negative results of these studies are in part due to limitations in their design and conduct, including numbers and similarities of patients randomized to prayer and no-prayer groups. As a theologian who has been engaged in spiritual healing, I would say these inconsistent and negative results are principally, if not entirely, due to a lack of connectedness through "authentic" compassion between those who prayed and those who were prayed for.

I believe that we should pray for spiritual healing with an attitude that enables us to communicate freely with God. Jesus taught right attitude, not right formula for prayer, especially when he said, "when you pray, go into your room, close the door, and pray to your Father, who is unseen."[33] A right or spiritually healthy attitude is viewed as an acceptance rather than an expectation of God, as a giving over rather than a giving up to God, and as being rather than doing in God's presence.[34] To get ourselves into this attitude, we must release ourselves from punishment theology and clear our minds of any other troublesome thoughts and emotions that can be obstacles to spiritual healing, such as fear, guilt, anger, remorse, jealousy, resentment, doubt, despair, and sorrow.[35] In a healing service, a guided meditation is a particularly effective means of creating the mental and spiritual stillness and openness necessary for connecting with God, and then praying to God for spiritual healing.

We should pray for spiritual healing with confidence, for as Jesus taught, "whatever you ask for in prayer, believe that you have received it, and it will be yours."[36] And, as Jesus clearly showed in his ministry, we should also pray humbly, with no thought or word being given to coercing God into healing, or telling God when and where to heal.[37]

I recommend that spontaneous prayer be encouraged when praying for a person's spiritual healing. Virtually all of the spontaneous prayers that I have heard in healing services have been appropriate and wonderful, reflecting authentic compassion for the person being prayed for. The words of these prayers have truly come from the heart, rather than from the mind!

Prayer can be specific, asking God to heal a particular illness. However, if specific prayer is used, the person being prayed for must consent to divulge the nature of his or her illness to others in the healing service. During specific prayer, the person being prayed for might place a hand, if possible, over the area of the body that is affected or most affected by her or his illness.[38] Prayer for spiritual healing can also be non-specific, asking God to heal using words such as "according to your will," and "let your will be done."[39] Every prayer for healing should acknowledge God's love for us and express our faith in God.[40]

A prayer for spiritual healing might include the phrase, "in the name of Jesus Christ." Jesus said, "to tell you the truth, my Father will give you whatever you ask in my name."[41] In Aramaic, the language that Jesus spoke, "in my name," was taken to mean, "as I would do it."[42] So when we say "in Jesus' name" or any other phrase invoking his name, we taking on the personality of Jesus, assuring God that we have the same understanding of God's nature and of the illness as Jesus would have had, and are praying as Jesus would have prayed.[43]

Many people believe that prayer for spiritual healing should include a request of the angelic realm for assistance in guiding divine healing energy. Angels serving as God's helpers figure prominently in the Bible, with their work being mentioned in over half of its books and in an equal number of books in the Old and New Testaments.[44] Their involvement with spiritual healing is reflected in the name of the prominent angel, Raphael, which in Hebrew means, "God heals."[45] These "spirits with a ministry"[46] have continued to intervene in history. Prominent theologians have proposed that we have at least one guardian angel or spirit guide, which is currently a belief held by the majority of Christians.[47] However, if we ask for angelic assistance with spiritual healing, actual experiences with the angels down through the ages suggests that we should call upon all angels, including spirit guides for their help.

Spiritual healing is usually a cumulative process, so that a single healing service may not be sufficient for a healing to occur.[48] Jesus' statement, "Ask and it will be given to you; seek and you will find; knock and the door will be opened to you,"[49] immediately follows a parable teaching persistence in knocking.[50] The duration and frequency of prayer for spiritual healing would particularly apply to chronic illness.[51] Therefore, not only should a healing service allow as much time as is possible to pray for each person who desires healing, but also the service should be conducted as regularly and as often as is possible.

As a way through which we connect with God for spiritual healing, prayer is the focal point of the healing service, when we ask God to send divine healing energy to heal others or us. Before we begin to pray for spiritual healing, we should get ourselves into a spiritually healthy attitude that enables us to communicate freely with God by releasing ourselves from punishment theology and clearing our minds of any troublesome thoughts and emotions that can be obstacles to spiritual healing. We should pray for spiritual healing confidently and humbly, making specific or non-specific requests for healing. Our prayers for spiritual healing should also acknowledge God's love for us and express our faith in God. A prayer for spiritual healing might include the phrase, "in the name of Jesus Christ," and ask for angelic assistance in guiding divine healing energy. Since spiritual healing is usually a process, healing services should be planned to allow ample time to pray for individual healing in one service, as well as in subsequent services.

Touch (The Laying on of Hands)

The laying on of hands for healing dates back to antiquity, known from writings found in India, Tibet, China, Egypt, and Greece.[52] Jesus used the laying on of hands effectively for spiritual healing, and told his disciples, "those who believe: In my name ... they will place their hands on sick people and they will get well."[53] However, the book of Acts describes only two instance of spiritual healing with the laying on of hands.[54] Moreover, the letter of James indicates that the early Church used anointing with oil rather than the laying on of hands in its practice of spiritual healing.[55]

I believe that the laying on of hands is a way of using our body's subtle energy system - the complex, highly-organized system of electromagnetic energy that exists within and around us - as a conduit for divine healing energy. Within us this energy flows along a network of pathways, or meridians,[56] and around us it exists as an energy field, or aura.[57] The aura has seven distinct layers, each of which is associated with our various physical, mental, emotional, or spiritual functions.[58] The aura and the physical body are penetrated through and through by seven, major cone-shaped vortices of energy, or chakras, each of which is associated with a particular auric layer.[59] The chakras receive energy from the universal energy field and transmit energy within the auric layers, thus vitalizing each auric layer and in turn the physical body.[60] The auric layers and chakras can be detected with our senses (e.g., as a tingling sensation in our hands, as a glow of various colors with our eyes). Our subtle energy system is generally believed to represent the essence of our soul, or spirit.[61]

Imbalances in levels of energy or blockages in the flow of energy in our subtle energy system cause illness and are caused by illness.[62] The subtle energy therapies of complementary and alternative medicine, such as acupuncture, Healing Touch and Reiki, detect and correct these imbalances and blockages, and thus aid in the prevention and the healing of illnesses.

During the laying on of hands for spiritual healing, our subtle energy system serves as a channel for the passage of divine healing energy to the person for whom we are praying, to bring about physical, mental, emotional, and spiritual healing. The flow of this energy is sometimes experienced as warmth or tingling in the hands of the person who is praying, and as warmth in the person on whom hands are placed.

The Church has revived the laying on of hands for spiritual healing over the past several decades. In current Roman Catholic liturgies for anointing of the sick, the priest lays his hands upon the head of each ill person in silence just after he anoints the person. In the current Protestant healing liturgies, either the minister or the minister and a small team of representatives of the church lay hands upon the ill person while praying for healing, which may be preceded by anointing of the person by the minister. Notably, the time given to the laying on of hands in these liturgies is usually a few seconds in duration for each ill person. I believe that this time is insufficient to generate optimal connectedness with God and each other for spiritual healing. Therefore, I suggest that every laying on of hands, accompanied by prayer, last a minimum of three minutes.

An ill person who desires spiritual healing, but is unable to attend a healing service, can be represented at the service by a surrogate, or stand-in, for the laying on of hands. The person being prayed for must give the surrogate permission to divulge the nature of his or her illness; otherwise, only non-specific prayer for healing should be used. When I know in advance of a service that an ill person will have a surrogate, I encourage the ill person to be in a prayerful attitude while the service is being held, so that his or her spirit can be fully open to receiving divine healing energy.

Everyone who attends a healing service should be invited to participate in the laying on of hands to maximize the flow of divine healing energy to the person being prayed for. Those who do not wish to participate in the laying on of hands should be asked to join in prayer or sit in meditation for healing.

Participants in the laying on of hands should comfortably surround and gently touch the ill person or a person in the line of contact with the ill person. When many attend a healing service, more than one location for performing the laying on of hands may be advisable to allow ample time to lay hands on and pray for each person who desires spiritual healing.

As a way through which we connect with God and each other for spiritual healing, the laying on of hands in a healing service enables us to serve as channels for the passage of divine healing energy to the ill person on whom our hands are placed. An ill person who is unable to attend a healing service can be represented by a surrogate, must give permission to the surrogate to divulge the nature of her or his illness, and should be encouraged to be in a prayerful attitude during the service. Everyone at a healing service should be invited to participate in the laying on of hands, while allowing ample time to lay hands on and pray for each person who desires spiritual healing.

Part IV

A Healing Service

Overview

In Part III, I described how the design and conduct of a healing service are shaped by spiritual faith, compassion, prayer and the laying on of hands. We should also give consideration to providing an ambiance for the service that helps to open people's minds and spirits to God's healing Spirit.

A healing service can take place anywhere, even out of doors. In a church it might be held in the sanctuary or chapel or, for small number of people, in a pleasantly decorated room with everyone seated in a circle. Indoors, the ambiance can be enhanced with soft lighting, including candles, and the playing of inspirational music before the service. Distractions during the service should be prevented by asking attendees to turn off their cell phones and pagers, closing the door or doors to where it is being held and placing a sign or signs for silence in the church entryway and hallways.

I recommend that everyone who comes to a healing service be provided a worship bulletin that contains all of readings, songs and prayers, and possibly the message, for many wish to keep the bulletin to read again. As a healing service begins, connectedness with God and each other can be intensified with words of inspiration, extending a warm welcome, describing what is to occur in the service, inviting all to welcome those around them in the spirit of love, and affirming the reality of spiritual healing in readings from scripture and in a message. A spiritually uplifting song might precede the message.

A guided meditation can also help us get into a spiritually healthy attitude for communicating freely with God for spiritual healing, by calming our minds and clearing them of troublesome thoughts and emotions. The words of a meditation should be spoken slowly and clearly, in a gentle voice that everyone can hear. The placement and duration of pauses should be sufficient to allow mental processing of each scene being described. In the "Resources" section I will give five examples of the kind of meditation that I use in a healing service. Other resources can be useful in selecting and developing guided meditations.[1]

I believe that a healing service should focus only on spiritual healing, and not serve as a means to something else, such as seeking God's forgiveness for sin. This service should give purpose and meaning to everything that is said and done. It should avoid such pitfalls as inappropriate emphasis on faith, teachings that induce guilt or anxiety, trivializing, judging, predicting how God will work, and making demands of God.

A framework for a healing service and resources for use in it follow. An example of a service is provided in Appendix C.

HEALING SERVICE

(Where)

(When)

Into God's Presence *(Background Music)*

Words of Inspiration *(Leader or Reader) (See Resources.)*

Welcome *(Leader)*

> A most warm welcome to everyone who has come to our healing service. With faith in God's love for us and in our love for God and each other, we have come together to pray for spiritual healing. First we will fully open our minds and spirits to God. Then those who desire spiritual healing of themselves or persons who are not here will be invited to come forwards, so that we may lay our hands upon them and pray for healing. The laying on of hands is an ancient, universal, religious practice for channeling the healing energy of the Holy Spirit to those who desire healing of themselves or others.
>
> I now invite you to welcome those around you in the spirit of love.

Scripture *(Leader or Reader) (See Resources.)*

> *The New Testament passages might be preceded by:*
>
> Jesus of Nazareth was a remarkable spiritual healer, and he commissioned his disciples to go out into the world to heal, as well as to teach and preach, as he did. Spiritual healing has continued in the Church to this day. In the following readings from the Gospels of _____ and _____, Jesus heals people who are

able and unable to come to him, as we will ask God to do in this healing service.

Song (All) *(See Resources.)*

Message *(Leader) (See Resources.)*

The message might be followed by:

Soon we will pray to God for the healing of those who are with us and for those who are not with us. Although the prayer that we use during the laying on of hands asks for healing "according to God's will," the person for whom we are praying may also wish that we pray for a specific healing.

Spiritual healing occurs when we humbly, sincerely, and trustingly ask God for help in healing our own or another person's illness. When we experience healing, we may find ourselves regaining physical, mental, emotional, and spiritual strength, being able to live with an illness and its effects, coming closer to God and loved ones, and feeling peace at the end of life. And, for some, healing can be so great that the illness is actually cured.

We may believe that God punishes us for our sins by making us ill. However, Jesus would tell us that God does not punish us with illness, but with unconditional love wants us to be whole in body, mind and spirit. So we should release the thought of illness being God's punishment from our minds.

The following guided meditation will also help us get into a spiritually healthy attitude for communicating freely with God for spiritual healing, by calming our minds and clearing them of troublesome thoughts and emotions.

Guided Meditation *(Leader or Reader) (See Resources.)*

Solo or Song (All) *(See Resources.)*

A Prayer for Healing (All) *(See Resources.)*

The Lord's Prayer (All) *("Trespasses ... trespass" or "sins ... sin" are preferred.)*

The Laying on of Hands

>(Those who do not participate in the laying on of hands are asked to join in prayer.)

>With hands being laid upon a person who desires his or her own healing

>(All) **As God loves us, we lay our hands upon you to help you receive divine healing energy. With faith in God** *(may add "and in the name of Jesus Christ")*, **we pray for your healing according to God's will.**

>(Additional prayers by individuals are invited.)

>With hands being laid upon a person who desires healing of another

>(All) **As God loves us, we lay our hands upon you to help you receive and send divine healing energy to _____. With faith in God (may add "and in the name of Jesus Christ"), we pray for his/her healing according to God's will.**

>(Additional prayers by individuals are invited.)

Prayer of Thankfulness (All) *(See Resources.)*

Parting Song (All) *(See Resources.)*

Benediction *(Leader)(See Resources.)*

Resources

Words of Inspiration

The LORD is my shepherd, I shall not be in want.
  He makes me lie down in green pastures,
he leads me beside quiet waters,
  he restores my soul.
He guides me in the paths of righteousness
  for his name's sake.
Even though I walk
  through the valley of the shadow of death,
I will fear no evil,
  for you are with me;
your rod and your staff,
  they comfort me.

Surely goodness and love will follow me
  all the days of my life,
and I will dwell in the house of the LORD forever.

Psalm 23:1-4, 6

I cried out to God for help;
  I cried out to God to hear me.
When I was in distress, I sought the Lord;
  at night I stretched out untiring hands
  and my soul refused to be comforted,

Then I thought, "To this I will appeal:
  the years of the right hand of the Most High."
I will remember the deeds of the LORD;
  yes, I will remember your miracles of long ago.
I will meditate on all your works
  and consider all your mighty deeds.

Psalm 77:1-2, 10-12

I lift my eyes up to the hills -
    where does my help come from?
My help comes from the LORD,
    the Maker of heaven and earth.
He will not let your foot slip -
    he who watches over you will not slumber;

The LORD watches over you -
    the LORD is your shade at your right hand;
the sun will not harm you by day,
    nor the moon by night.

The LORD will keep you from all harm -
    he will watch over your life;
the LORD will watch over your coming and   going
    both now and forevermore.

Psalm 121:1-3, 5-8

Do you not know?
    Have you not heard?
The LORD is the everlasting God,
    the Creator of the ends of the earth.
He will not grow tired or weary,
    and his understanding no one can fathom.
He gives strength to the weary
    and increases the power of the weak.
Even youths grow tired and weary,
    and young men stumble and fall;
but those who hope in the LORD
    will renew their strength.
They will soar on wings like eagles;
    they will run and not grow weary,
    they will walk and not be faint.

Isaiah 40:28-31

Shout for joy, O heavens;
    rejoice, O earth;
    burst into song, O mountains!
For the Lord comforts his people
    and will have compassion on his
    afflicted ones.

Isaiah 49:13

Jesus said, "Ask and it will be given to you; seek and you will find; knock and the door will be opened unto you. For everyone who asks receives; he who seeks finds; and to him who knocks, the door will be opened."

Matthew 7:7-8

Jesus said, "I tell you the truth, if anyone says to this mountain, 'Go, through yourself into the sea,' and does not doubt in his heart but believes that what he says will happen, it will be done for him. Therefore, I tell you, whatever you ask for in prayer, believe that you have received it, and it will be yours."

Mark 11:23-24

The apostle Paul wrote, "Praise be to God and Father of our Lord Jesus Christ, the Father of compassion and the God of all comfort, who comforts us in all our troubles, so that we can comfort those in any trouble with the comfort we ourselves have received from God."

2 Corinthians 1:3-4

The apostle Paul wrote, "Do not be anxious about anything, but in everything, by prayer and petition, with thanksgiving, present yourselves to God. And the peace that passes all understanding, will guard your hearts and minds in Jesus Christ."

Philippians 4:6-7

James, traditionally identified as the brother of Jesus, wrote, "Is any one of you sick? He should call the elders of the church to pray over him and anoint him with oil in the name of the Lord. And the prayer offered in faith will make the sick person well; the Lord will raise him up."

James 5:14-15

Good people,
Most royal greening verdancy,
Rooted in the sun,
You shine with radiant light.
In this circle of earthly existence
You shine so finely,
It surpasses understanding.
God hugs you.
You are encircled by the arms
of the mystery of God.

Hildegard of Bingen[2]

Let nothing disturb you,
let nothing dismay you.
All things pass
God never changes.
Patience attains all that it strives for.
Those who have God
find they lack for nothing.
God alone suffices.

Teresa of Avila[3]

O Hidden Life, vibrant in every atom,
O Hidden Light, shining in every creature,
O Hidden Love, embracing all in Oneness,
May we who feel ourselves as one with You
Know we are therefore one with every other.

Annie Besant[4] *(adapted)*

Like you, I have been here since the beginning, and shall be to the end of days. There is no ending to my existence.

For the human soul is but part of a burning torch which God separated from the divine self at the beginning of Creation.

Thus my soul and your soul are one, and we are one with God.

Kahlil Gibran[5] (adapted)

You carry the cure within you.
Everything that comes your way is blessed.
The Creator gives you one more day.
Stand on the neck of Fearful Mind.

Do not wait to open your heart.
Let yourself go into the Mystery.
Sometimes the threads have no weave.
The price of not loving yourself is high.

Jim Cohn[6]

You could make this place alive,
divine, infused with inner light.
You can take your shy, secret hopes
and construct them into what they might.

The place can be anywhere.
The only source is within you.
All that you see was once a dream.
Dream again today and that you do become.

Barry Harris[7]

May we learn to open in love
so all the doors and windows
of our bodies swing wide
on their rusty hinges.

May we learn to give ourselves with both hands,
to lift each other on our shoulders,
to carry one another along.

May holiness move in us
so we may pay attention to its small voice
and honor its light in each other.

Dawna Markova[8]

Thy name is our healing, O our God,
     and remembrance of Thee is our remedy.
Nearness to Thee is our hope,
     and love for Thee is our compassion.
Thy mercy to us
     is our healing and our succor
     in both this world and the world to come.
Thou, verily, art the All-Bountiful,
     the All-Knowing, the All-Wise.

Baha'u'llah (adapted)[9]

Every
Child
Has known God,
Not the God of names,
Not the God of don'ts,
Not the God who ever does
Anything weird,
But the God who only knows four words
And keeps repeating them, saying:
"Come dance with Me."
Come
Dance.

Hafiz[10]

God's love shines brightly,
Fully revealing,
Wholly embracing,
As we pray for healing.

God's love shines brightly,
Given graciously,
Received thankfully,
As we pray for healing.

Doug Busby

Scripture

<u>Elijah revives the widow's son</u>
Some time later the son of the woman who owned the house became ill. He grew worse and worse, and finally stopped breathing. She said to Elijah, "What you have against me, man of God? Did you come to me to remind me of my sin and kill my son?" "Give me your son," Elijah replied. He took him from her arms, carried him to the upper room where he was staying, and laid him on his bed. Then he cried out to the LORD, "O LORD my God, have you brought tragedy also upon the widow I am staying with, by causing her son to die?" Then he stretched himself out upon the boy three times and cried out to the LORD, "O LORD my God, let this boy's life return to him!" The LORD heard Elijah's cry, and the boy's life returned to him and he lived.

1 Kings 17:17-22

<u>Elisha cures Naaman, the commander of a foreign army, of leprosy</u>
So Naaman went with his horses and chariots and stopped at the door of Elisha's house. Elisha sent a messenger to say to him, "Go, wash yourself seven times in the Jordan, and your flesh will be restored and you will be cleansed." But Naaman went away

angry and said, "I thought that he would surely come out to me and call on the name of LORD his God, wave his hand over the spot and cure me of my leprosy! Are not Abana and Pharpar, the rivers of Damascus, better than any of the waters of Israel? Couldn't I wash in them and be cleansed?" So he turned and went off in a rage. Namaan's servants went to him and said, "My father, if the prophet had told you to do some great thing, would you not have done it? How much more, then, when he tells you, 'Wash and be cleansed'!" So he went down and dipped himself in the Jordan seven times, as the man of God had told him, and his flesh was restored and became clean like that of a young boy.

2 Kings 5:9-14

Jesus heals a man with leprosy, who is able to come to him
When he [Jesus] came down from the mountainside, large crowds followed him. A man with leprosy came and knelt before him and said, "Lord, if you are willing, you can make me clean." Jesus reached out his hand and touched the man. "I am willing," he said. "Be clean!" Immediately he was cured of his leprosy.

Matthew 8:1-3

Other examples: Mark 7:32-35 (healing of a deaf and mute man), Luke 13:10-14 (healing of a crippled woman); John 9:1-7 (healing of a man born blind)

Jesus heals the royal official's son, who is unable to come to him
Once more he [Jesus] visited Cana in Galilee, where he had turned the water into wine. And there was a certain royal official whose son lay sick at Capernaum. When this man heard that Jesus had arrived in Galilee from Judea, he went to him and

begged him to come and heal his son, who was close to death. "Unless you people see miraculous signs and wonders," Jesus said, "you will never believe." The royal official said, "Sir, come down before my child dies." Jesus replied, "You may go. Your son will live." The man took Jesus at his word and departed. While he was still on the way, his servants met him with the news that his boy was living. When he inquired as to the time when his son got better, they said to him, "The fever left him yesterday at the seventh hour." Then the father realized that this was the exact time at which Jesus said to him, "Your son will live." So he and all of his household believed.

John 4:46-53

Another example: Matthew 8:5-13 (healing of the Centurion's servant of paralysis).

Peter heals the paralytic at Lydda

As Peter traveled about the country, he went to visit the saints in Lydda. There he found a man named Aeneas, a paralytic who had been bedridden for eight years. "Aeneas," Peter said to him, "Jesus Christ heals you. Get up and take care of your mat." Immediately Aeneas got up.

Acts 9:32-34

Paul heals the father of the chief official of the island of Malta

There was an estate nearby that belonged to Publius, the chief official of the island [of Malta]. He welcomed us to his home and for three days entertained us hospitably. His father was sick in bed, suffering from fever and dysentery. Paul went in to see him and, after prayer, placed his hands upon him and healed him.

Acts 28:7-8

All people that on earth do dwell,[11]
sing out your faith with cheerful voice;
Delight in God whose praise you tell,
whose presence calls you to rejoice.

Know that there is one God indeed,
who fashions us without our aid,
Who claims us, gives us all we need,
whose tender care will never fade.

Precious Lord, take my hand,[12]
lead me on, let me stand,
I am tired, I am weak, I am worn;
Through the storm, through the night,
lead me on to the light:
Take my hand, precious Lord, lead me home.

O Holy Spirit, Root of life,[13]
Creator, cleanser of all things,
anoint our wounds, awaken us
with lustrous movement of your wings.

O Holy Wisdom, Soaring Power,
encompass us with wings unfurled
and carry us, encircling all,
above, below, and through the world.

Spirit of the Living God, fall afresh on me.[14]
Spirit of the living God, fall afresh on me.
Melt me, mold me, fill me, use me.
Spirit of the living God, fall afresh on me.

Breathe on me, Breath of God,[15]
fill me with life anew,

that I may love the way you love,
and do what you would do.

Breathe on me Breath of God,
stir in me one desire:
That every earthly part of me
may glow with earthly fire.

For the beauty of the earth,[16]
for the splendor of the skies,
for the love which from our birth,
over and around us lies,
God of all, to you we raise
this our song of grateful praise.

For the joy of human love,
brother, sister, parent, child,
friends on earth, and friends above,
for all gentle thoughts and mild,
God of all, ...

This little light of mine,[17]
I'm gonna let it shine.
This little light of mine,
I'm gonna let it shine.
This little light of mine,
I'm gonna let it shine,
Let it shine, let it shine, let it shine.

Amazing grace, how sweet the sound[18]
that saved a soul like me!
I once was lost, but now am found,
was blind but now I see.

My God has promised good to me,
whose word my hope secures;
God will my shield and portion be
as long as life endures.

Open my eyes, that I may see[19]
glimpses of truth thou hast for me;
place in my hands the wonderful key
that shall unclasp and set me free.
Silently now I wait for thee
ready, my God, thy will to see.
Open my eyes, illumine me,
Spirit divine!

Open my ears, that I may hear
voices of truth thou sendest clear;
and while the wave-notes fall on my ear,
everything false will disappear.
Silently now ...

Open my mouth, and let me bear
gladly the warm truth everywhere;
open my heart and let me prepare
love with thy children thus to share.
Silently now ...

Come forth, O Love divine,[20]
seek now this soul of mine,
and visit it with your own ardor glowing;
O Comforter, draw near,
within my heart appear,
and kindle it, your holy flame bestowing.

And so the yearning strong
with which the soul; will long,
shall far out-pass the power of human telling;
For none can guess its grace,
till love create a place
wherein the Holy Spirit makes a dwelling.

Messages

Example 1

Jesus said, "Ask and it will be given to you; seek and you will find; knock and the door will be opened unto you. For everyone who asks receives; he who seeks finds; and to him who knocks, the door will be opened." (Matthew 7:7-8).

When we knock on a door to ask the person who opens it for something, we must be prepared to communicate our request openly and clearly. Therefore, when we knock on the door to the heavenly realm to ask God for spiritual healing, we must be prepared to pray in the same ways. This preparation involves focusing our minds and spirits on connecting with God in prayer, or as Jesus said, getting into the right attitude for prayer. This is what we are doing as we prepare to pray for the spiritual healing of those who are with us and not with us.

Do we need reassurance that spiritual healing still occurs? If so, we can look back at the historical reality of spiritual healing and even listen to persons who have experienced it. But whether or not we need this reassurance, Jesus is telling us that when we really believe that prayer for healing works, it will!

(See additional paragraphs under Framework.)

Example 2

Jesus said, "I tell you the truth, if anyone says to this mountain, 'Go, throw yourself into the sea,' and does not doubt in his heart but believes that what he says will happen, it will be done for him. Therefore I tell you, whatever you ask for in prayer, believe that you have received it, and it will be yours." (Mark 11:23-24.)

In these verses from the Gospel of Mark, Jesus is reassuring his disciples about the power of prayer, as he gives them the knowledge and experience necessary to carry on his ministry, including spiritual healing, when he is no longer with them. We might wonder: Why did Jesus have to give the disciples this reassurance when, according to the Gospels, he had already empowered them for spiritual healing and sent them out to heal with remarkable success? An appropriate answer to this question might be that Jesus' disciples, being ordinary people like us, were prone to need reassurance of God's love and support while being trained for such a challenging ministry.

Do we need to have at least some reassurance that spiritual healing still occurs? If so, we can look back at the long history of spiritual healing and even listen to persons who have experienced it. But whether or not we need this reassurance, Jesus is telling us that when we really believe that prayer for healing works, it will!

(See additional paragraphs under Framework.)

Example 3

A traditional Hebrew prayer[21] suggests that angels can be all around us:

In the Name of God the Almighty,
To my right Michael, and to my left Gabriel,
And before me Uriel, and behind me Raphael,
And over my head, the presence of God.

Human beings have always had an interest in certain spiritual beings, to whom God has given special responsibilities in heaven and on earth. We call them "angels," which comes from the ancient Hebrew word for "messengers from God." The names of some of these angels, such as Michael, Gabriel, Uriel, and Raphael, are quite familiar to Jews, Christians, and Muslims alike.

Through the ages - especially in the past century - numerous people have described their being assisted from danger to safety by spirit beings. Many call these beings their "guardian angels" or "spirit guides." Moreover, many people, particularly those who have worked extensively with spiritual healing, have sensed that they can also help us from sickness to health by knowing what we are suffering from, and then "guiding" God's healing energy to help correct it. Interestingly, the name, Raphael, translates from Hebrew to English as, "God heals."

Whether or not we believe that angels can help God in healing us physically, mentally, emotionally and spiritually, we know that only God makes spiritual healing possible for us. And even though we may pray to God, or both to God and angels for healing, we must then "let go and let God" help us with our healing.

(See additional paragraphs under Framework.)

Example 4

Dom Hélder Câmera, the great Roman Catholic archbishop who expressed deep concern for the poor of Brazil, wrote the following poem:[22]

> When I was a youngster
>   I wanted to go out running
>   among the mountain peaks.
> And when, between two summits
>   a gap appeared,
>   why not leap across the chasm?
> Led by the angel's hand,
>   all my life long
>   this is what happened,
>   this, exactly.

This wonderful poem reminds us that when we were youngsters, we believed that we could overcome life's problems if we really set our minds to it. But as adults we soon learned that usually we can resolve these problems, and that sometimes we need help in overcoming them.

A serious illness of the body, mind or spirit can prevent us from living a creative and joyful life. Yet, as the archbishop's poem says, a divine hand is always available to help us overcome whatever problem faces us. And so we reach out to God in prayer, asking for divine healing energy to help us with our healing.

(See additional paragraphs under Framework.)

Example 5

Amelia Earhart, the great female aviator of the 1930's, wrote the following poem:[23]

> Courage is the price that life exacts
>> for granting peace.
> The soul that knows it not,
>> knows no release
>> from the little things;
> Knows not the livid loneliness of fear,
>> nor mountain heights
>> where bitter joy can hear
>> the sound of wings.

Amelia Earhart was a great pioneer in aviation, facing many challenges in flying airplanes record-breaking distances. In 1937 her last and greatest challenge - flying around the world - ended tragically somewhere in the South Pacific, with no one ever knowing what happened to her.

In this wonderful poem Amelia is giving us a clear message. She is saying that we need to have courage in order to overcome life's challenges, most especially the "livid loneliness of fear." How fittingly her words echo what we experience when challenged by illness. We certainly can be fearful and lack courage! But we can overcome our fear and generate courage with the certain knowledge that God wishes us to be whole physically, mentally, emotionally and spiritually, and can help us heal.

(See additional paragraphs under Framework.)

Guided Meditations

<u>Example 1</u>

Let us prepare ourselves for a guided meditation by relaxing comfortably in our chairs, with our hands apart on our laps and our feet flat on the floor. Now close your eyes, and breathe slowly and deeply three times, in through your nose and out through your mouth. *(Accompany the breathing exercise with "in through your nose and out through your mouth.")*

Imagine that you are taking a drive alone in the country on a warm summer afternoon, to enjoy a few moments of peace in this hustle-bustle world. Lost in thought you turn onto a road that takes you into a dense forest that is unfamiliar to you. *(Pause)* As you slow the car, wondering where you are, you notice a narrow, winding path going into the forest, with a small sign posted next to it. You stop and back the car to read the sign, which in golden letters announces, "Sanctuary, Welcome!" Curious as to what this sign means and where the path goes, you park the car by the side of the road, get out of it, and begin to walk on the path. *(Pause)*

You find the cool, fresh air of the forest soothing. You smell many wonderful fragrances coming from the bed of brightly-colored flowers bordering the path as it winds though the forest. You look upwards and see that the trees frame a rich blue sky, making its few puffy clouds seem even whiter. You hear birds singing to each other all around you. "What a wonderful place" you say to yourself, as you become even more inquisitive and decide to continue walking. *(Pause)*

After several minutes you come upon an open space in the forest - a small meadow of ankle-deep grass, swaying gently back and forth. You walk out of the forest into the meadow to enjoy the simple beauty of the grass below you, the trees around you and the sky above you. *(Pause)*. You realize that you could be enjoying this moment even more if your mind could be clear of concerns and emotions that are bothering you.

While standing in the meadow, you feel a warm wind on your face, as though a gentle hand is touching it. You hear an inner voice tell you that the wind can carry away troublesome thoughts and emotions. The voice says that for this, all you need to do is to take in a deep breath, and each time as you breathe out, say to yourself what troublesome thought or emotion you are releasing into the wind. So you take a deep breath, and as you breathe out, you say to yourself, "I release all of my fear into the wind." *(Pause)* You take another deep breath and as you breathe out, you say to yourself, "I release all of my guilt into the wind." *(Pause)* *(Repeat separately for anger, resentment, remorse, jealousy, doubt, despair, sorrow, etc.) (Pause)*

You now feel that you are in a state of mental, emotional, and spiritual peace, cleansed of all troublesome thoughts and emotions. You give thanks to God for this wonderful experience. *(Pause)*

You walk back through the forest on the winding path, stopping for a moment to smell the flowers, look up through the trees at the sky, and listen to the birds. *(Pause)* You leave the forest and its welcoming sign, get into your car, and drive away.

You may open your eyes when you wish. *(Pause)*

(A variation on this meditation might be to replace the meadow with a pool of clear, warm water. A troublesome thought or emotion is washed away with each immersion in the water.)

Example 2

Let us prepare ourselves for a guided meditation by relaxing comfortably in our chairs, with our hands apart on our laps and our feet flat on the floor. Now close your eyes, and breathe slowly and deeply three times, in through your nose and out through your mouth. *(Accompany the breathing exercise with "in through your nose and out through your mouth.")*

Imagine that you are sitting alone on a bench under a tall maple tree, on a mild spring day. The bench is beside a tranquil pond upon which two swans are slowly gliding back and forth, barely making a ripple. The leaves on the tree are not yet in full bloom, allowing the warmth of the sun to come through its branches. Far overhead a hawk swings lazily back and forth in the deep blue sky. *(Pause)* In this place of serenity you begin to feel close to God, and wonder, "Would God hear me if I pray?" But as you begin to say a prayer, you find that some concerns and emotions are blocking the way to finding the right words to say. *(Pause)*

You are startled by a soft, male voice coming from behind you asking, "Would you mind if I also sit on the bench?" You turn around and see a smiling young man in jogging clothes and slightly out of breath. "Yes," you say. *(Pause)*

As the man sits down on the bench, he introduces himself as Christopher, and you reply with your name. You feel compelled to engage him in conversation and soon realize that he is very concerned about your mental and spiritual wellbeing. "Who is this remarkable person?" you begin to wonder. *(Pause)*

After several minutes of chatting with Christopher, he suggests that you close your eyes, and in your mind ask him to remove any concerns or emotions that are bothering you. You are surprised by his unexpected suggestion, but an inner voice tells you to "Trust him." And so with eyes closed, you say in your mind to him, "Please remove my fear," *(Pause)*. Then you say in your mind to him, "Please remove my guilt," *(Pause)* *(Repeat separately for anger, resentment, remorse, jealousy, doubt, despair, sorrow, etc.) (Pause)*

Christopher softly asks, "How are you now?" You realize that your mind and spirit are now at peace and you joyfully reply, "Wonderful, thank you!" *(Pause)* As Christopher gets up to leave, he gently grasps your hands in his, and says, "Good, now you can freely talk with God." As he jogs into the distance, you feel ready and able to pray. *(Pause)*

You may open your eyes when you wish. *(Pause)*

(A variation on this meditation might be to replace "Christopher" with "your guardian angel").

Example 3

Let us prepare ourselves for a guided meditation by relaxing comfortably in our chairs, with our hands apart on our laps and our feet flat on the floor. Now close your eyes, and breathe slowly and deeply three times, in through your nose and out through your mouth. *(Accompany the breathing exercise with "in through your nose and out through your mouth.")*

Imagine that you are alone on a beach on a warm summer day, walking barefoot over a stretch of sand kept moist by small waves washing up on the shore. To your right the dark blue water stretches to the horizon, where it blends with the cloudless blue sky. And to your left small dunes of fine rippled sand are capped by tall grass swaying in the gentle breeze. *(Pause)*

You stop and look about you at the water, sky and sand, and momentarily experience a sense of being at peace. *(Pause)* You ask yourself, "Why can't I feel this way all the time? *(Pause)* Almost immediately an inner voice replies: "Because your mind is cluttered with so many troublesome thoughts and emotions." *(Pause)* Then the voice tells you, "Go to the water's edge and write a concern or emotion that is bothering you in the moist sand, and let a wave come and wash it away." *(Pause)*

You pick up a small, smooth stick, and kneel at the water's edge. As a wave recedes, you write in the sand, "fear," which is washed away by the next wave. *(Pause)* Then you write, "guilt," which is washed away by the next wave. *(Pause)* *(Repeat separately for anger, resentment, remorse, jealousy, doubt, despair, sorrow, etc.) (Pause)*

When you have nothing more to write in the sand and be washed away, you realize that you are again experiencing the sense of peace, and that this time it does not go away. You continue walking along the beach, enjoying its beauty. *(Pause)*

You may open your eyes when you wish. *(Pause)*

(A variation of this meditation might be to write each troublesome thought or emotion in the sand of a dune to be blown away by the wind.)

Example 4

Let us prepare ourselves for a guided meditation by relaxing comfortably in our chairs, with our hands apart on our laps and our feet flat on the floor. Now close your eyes, and breathe slowly and deeply three times, in through your nose and out through your mouth. *(Accompany the breathing exercise with "in through your nose and out through your mouth.")*

Imagine that a point of golden energy is appearing in the air above you, and then slowly expanding and descending until it gently touches the top of your head. *(Pause)* Feel the pleasant warmth of this energy touch you and pass downwards through your entire body - your head and neck, your shoulders and arms, your chest and abdomen, your pelvis and legs, and through the soles of your feet into the Earth.. *(Pause)*

You hear an inner voice invite you to release any troublesome thoughts or emotions into the flow of golden energy, to be carried down into the Earth. You do so, and say to yourself, "I release all of my fear." *(Pause)* Then you say to yourself, "I release all of my guilt." *(Pause)* (*Repeat separately for anger, resentment, remorse, jealousy, doubt, despair, sorrow, etc.) (Pause)*

The ball of golden energy seems to know when you have no more to troublesome thoughts or emotions to release. It slowly ascends and contracts, and disappears in the air above you, leaving you with a deep sense of peace *(Pause)*

You may open your eyes when you wish. *(Pause)*

<u>Example 5</u>

Let us prepare ourselves for a guided meditation by relaxing comfortably in our chairs, with our hands apart on our laps and our feet flat on the floor. Now close your eyes, and breathe slowly and deeply three times, in through your nose and out through your mouth. *(Accompany the breathing exercise with "in through your nose and out through your mouth.")*

Imagine that you are with several of your friends, sitting around a campfire. After sharing several stories, everyone becomes quiet, gazing into the fire. *(Pause)* You feel the gentle warmth of the fire, hear the crackling of the burning wood, and are entranced by multicolored flames rising to release golden sparks into the dark night air. *(Pause)* Soon you realize that you could be enjoying this moment more if your mind could be free of troublesome thoughts and emotions. You share this with the others, and most say that they feel the same way. *(Pause)*

One of your friends suggests a way to rid the mind of troublesome thoughts and emotions. She hands a pencil and small pad of paper to each person around the fire. She suggests writing one troublesome thought or emotion at a time on the pad, gazing at the word or words for a few seconds, and then tearing the paper off the pad and throwing it into the fire. You write "fear" on the pad, look at this word for a few seconds, tear the paper off the pad, and throw it into the fire. *(Pause)* Then you write "guilt" on the pad, look at this word for a few seconds, tear the paper off the pad, and throw it into the fire. *(Pause)* *(Repeat separately for anger, remorse, jealousy, doubt, despair, sorrow, etc.) (Pause)*

When you have no more troublesome thoughts or emotions to be consumed in the fire, you realize that you are experiencing a sense of peace. You can now fully enjoy this wonderful moment. *(Pause)*

You may open your eyes when you wish. *(Pause)*

Prayers for Healing

Lord, make me an instrument of your peace,
Where there is hatred, let me sow love.
Where there is injury, let me sow pardon.
Where there is discord, let me sow unity.
Where there is doubt, let me sow faith.
Where there is despair, let me sow hope.
Where there is sadness, let me sow joy.
Where there is darkness, let me sow light.

O Divine Master, grant that I may not so much seek
    to be consoled as to console.
To be understood, as to understand.
To be loved, as to love.
For it is in the giving, that we receive.
It is in the pardoning, that we are pardoned.
It is in dying, that we are born to eternal life.

Saint Francis of Assisi[24]

Lay your hands gently upon us,
let their touch render your peace,
let them bring your love and healing.
Lay your hands, gently lay your hands.

You were sent to free the broken-hearted,
You were sent to give sight to the blind,
You desire to heal all our illness.
Lay your hands, gently lay your hands.

Lord, we come to you through one another.
Lord, we come to you in all our need.
Lord, we come to you seeking wholeness,
Lay your hands, gently lay your hands.

Rita J. Donovan[25] *(adapted)*

This is a prayer for
the illumination of the body
    the body of the earth
    which is our rock and breath
    the body of the self
        which is the shining
        eternal strand
        of the soul
    the body of material substance which
        is the ancient gentle
        temple of the spirit.

May you move your divine hand
across us in each of these planes,
allowing the earth
of our bodies
and the ether
of our souls
to become fit grand vessels
for your own and our own
illustrious light.

Daphne Rose Kingma[26]

O Christ of the road
    of the wounded
O Christ of the tears
    of the broken
In me and with me
    the needs of the world
Grant us our prayers
    of loving and hoping
Grant us our prayers
    of yearning and healing.

J. Philip Newell[27] *(adapted)*

Hear our prayers O Lord. You who are the giver of
life and health: Send your blessing on all here present
who seek healing in mind, body and spirit. We trust

in you, Lord, who knows our hearts as we stand before you desiring wholeness.

Linda L. Smith[28]

O God, we humbly to ask you to heal those for whom we pray. Our spirits are fully open, ready to connect in love with you and each other for your timeless gift of spiritual healing.

Doug Busby

We thank you, God of all Creation, for your love for us. As Jesus Christ healed and taught his disciples to heal, we come together for spiritual healing in his name. Bless us in this time and place with your Spirit, for our healing and the healing of others.

Doug Busby

Loving God, we come to you in our love for you and each other, to ask that you bless those for whom we pray with the healing energy of your Spirit. Use us as you wish, as channels for your healing grace.

Doug Busby

All-powerful God, source of all healing, make those for whom we pray for healing fully aware of your presence with them. Open their eyes that they may see you; open their ears that they hear you; open their hearts that they may know your love. Cast the light of your Spirit upon them, so that they may be healed in body, mind, and spirit.

Doug Busby

Gracious God, your gift to us of faith in you assures us that you hear and answer our prayers for healing. So in the name of Jesus Christ we earnestly ask you to send us the healing energy of your Spirit, to heal those for whom we pray.

Doug Busby

Prayers of Thankfulness

Loving God, we are deeply thankful that you have listened to our prayers for healing and have provided the healing energy of your Spirit to those for whom we have prayed. We humbly ask that you continue to send them your gift of healing.

Doug Busby

O God, we are profoundly grateful for the healing that you have provided to those for whom we have prayed. We earnestly pray that you will continue to grace them with your healing Spirit, as they seek wholeness of body, mind, and spirit.

Doug Busby

Loving God, we give you our heartfelt thanks for answering our prayers for healing. We pray that the healing energy of your Spirit will remain with those for whom we have prayed.

Doug Busby

God of all love, we are profoundly thankful that you have heard our prayers and have blessed us with healing of body, mind, and spirit. We humbly ask that you will continue to assist back to health those for whom we have prayed.

Doug Busby

We thank you, God, for blessing all of us with divine healing energy. We pray that you will help us to be constantly mindful of your unconditional love for us, and your desire that we be whole in body, mind and spirit.

Doug Busby

Parting Songs

God be with you till we meet again;[29]
By good counsel guide, uphold you,
With a shepherd's care enfold you:
God be with you till we meet again.
Till we meet, till we meet,
till we meet at Jesus' feet;
till we meet, till we meet,
God be with you till we meet again.

God, dismiss us with your blessing;[30]
Fill our hearts with joy and peace;
Let us each your love possessing,
Give us still your healing grace;
Oh, refresh us, oh refresh us,
traveling through this wilderness.

God be with you, God be with you,[31]
God be with you till we meet again.
O God be with you, God be with you,
God be with you till we meet again.

Blest be the tie that binds[32]
our hearts in Christian love;
The fellowship of kindred minds
is like to that above.

When we are called to part,
it gives us inward pain;
But we shall be joined in heart,
and hope to meet again.

Alleluia, alleluia, alleluia, alleluia,[33]
Alleluia, alleluia, alleluia, alleluia.

Benedictions

As we leave this place, we commend ourselves to God's everlasting care, ever mindful of God's healing presence in our lives.

Doug Busby

Be assured of God's unceasing love.
God is always ready to hear us
and is always ready to heal us,
Whenever we pray for healing.

Doug Busby

God's gift of spiritual healing is been graciously given and thankfully received. God heals those for whom we pray. We are blessed by God!

Doug Busby

May God our Creator,
    the Source of all love,
    the Source of all healing,
    bless us with peace and joy,
    now and always.

Doug Busby

In our coming together for spiritual healing, we have connected with God and each other through faith, compassion, prayer, and the laying on of hands. We have truly been blessed with the healing energy of God's Spirit. May we go forth with confidence that with unconditional love, God will always provide this wonderful gift to us.

Doug Busby

Part V

Experience with the Healing Service

I have led the healing service described in this book in various church settings, often assisted by other clergy. When a healing service is new to a congregation, I have recommended that its purpose and content be described to the congregation prior to the service in a sermon on prayer for healing or in a seminar on spiritual healing. Healing services have also been announced in worship bulletins and community newspapers.

As persons arrive for a healing service in a church sanctuary or chapel, they have been handed a worship bulletin for the service and ushered to the most forward open pews. Based on the number of people expected to attend a service, one or more chairs for those who wish to receive the laying on of hands have been placed several feet apart at the sanctuary or chapel floor level in front of the first pew.

I have also led this healing service in the chapel of our local hospital, usually assisted by the hospital's director of spiritual care. The service has been held on a Wednesday every month, at 3:00 p.m. and 7:00 p.m., which have been the most convenient times both for hospital visitors and employees. Healing services have been announced through the hospital's internal e-mail and public address systems, on tented cards on cafeteria tables, and on the message board at the chapel entrance.

The hospital's spiritual care director and I have respected the religious diversity of those attending a healing service by omitting Scripture on Jesus' healing ministry, The Lord's Prayer, and "in the name of Jesus Christ" in prayers. People coming to the service have been given a worship bulletin and seated in a circle of chairs, with one chair remaining empty for those who wish to receive the laying on of hands.

When many persons have attended a healing service, several have usually come forward at different times to participate in the laying on of hands. Only a few people have preferred to remain seated in prayer throughout the laying on of hands.

The number of ill persons for whom we have prayed in a healing service has been about equally divided between those who are present and those who are not present. When people have represented one or more ill persons as surrogates, the laying on of hands is done and prayers are said separately for each ill person. I have concluded (and signaled) the end of each laying on of hands with a brief prayer of thanks for the healing that God has given to the person for whom we have prayed.

Finally, many of the hospital's employees said that they wished that they could attend a healing service during work hours, but the duration of it prevented them from doing so. Therefore, the hospital's director of spiritual care and I have also held an abbreviated, twenty-minute healing service, which we have called "A Twenty-Minute Gathering for Spiritual Healing," on a Thursday of every month. An example of this service, which is given to the leader and reader rather than being printed for all attendees, is provided in Appendix D.

Many people who have attended the healing service have described an intense feeling of connectedness with God and each other, and the presence of God's healing Spirit, especially during the laying on of hands. They have said that various parts of the service preceding the laying on of hands helped them to be open to these experiences, such as words about spiritual healing, the general prayer for healing, the guided meditation, and the invitation to participate in the laying on of hands.

Unusual sensations and spontaneous tearing have often occurred in the healing service, especially during the laying on of hands. The sensations have included warmth or tingling in the hands, a rush of warmth or tingling passing through the body, and momentary lightheadedness. Many who have just received the laying on of hands have been unsteady for a few seconds after standing up, and some have even needed assistance in walking back to where they had been sitting. Spontaneous embracing has often occurred immediately after laying on of hands and at the end of the service.

Occasionally when the healing service has been held in a church sanctuary, a snapping or crackling similar to the sound of electrical static has been heard for several seconds during the laying on of hands. This sound has come from various directions, usually high overhead, and has had no visible cause. I believe that it could have been created by the energy of the Holy Spirit.

Many have said that they have been touched by the healing energy of God's Spirit during the healing service. They have described accelerated healing, lessening of physical, mental, emotional and spiritual distress, and remission of cancer. Although I have listened to their wonderful stories of healing with intense interest, for me to retell them here would be beyond the scope of this book.

Appendix A

Spiritual Healing by Jesus[*]

Illnesses Healed	Sources	How Jesus Healed
Evil spirit possessing a man in the synagogue in Capernaum.	Mk. 1:23-26 Lk. 4:33-35	Jesus said to the spirit, "Be quiet!" and "Come out of him!" (Mk. 1:25)
Fever in Peter's mother-in-law.	Mk. 1:30-31 Mt. 8:14-15 Lk. 4:38-39	Jesus rebuked the fever, touched her and took her hand and helped her up.
Demonic possessions of and various sicknesses in many.	Mk. 1:32-33 Mt. 8:16 Lk. 4:40-41	Not described.
Demonic possession of many in Galilee	Mk. 1:39	Not described.
Leprosy in a man	Mk. 1:40-42 Mt. 8:2-3 Lk. 5:12-13	"Filled with compassion, Jesus reached out his hand and touched the man" and said, "Be clean!" (Mk. 1:41)
Paralysis in a man that made him bedridden.	Mk. 2:3-12 Mt. 9:2-7 Lk. 5:17-25	Jesus said to the man, "Son, your sins are forgiven," and then, "I tell you, get up, take your mat and go home." (Mk. 1:5, 11)
Withered hand of a man in the synagogue	Mk. 3:1-5 Mt. 12:9-13 Lk. 6:6-10	Jesus said to the man, "Stretch out your hand." (Mk. 3:5)
Diseases and unclean spirit possessions in crowds near the lake.	Mk. 3:9-11 Mt. 12:15	Not described.
An evil spirit ("many," according to this spirit) possessing a man in the region of the Gerasenes.	Mk. 5:2-13 Mt. 8:28-32 Lk. 8:27-33	Jesus said, "Come out of this man, you evil spirit!" (Mk. 5:8) He then sent the spirits into a herd of pigs, saying, "Go!" (Mt. 8:32)
Assumed death of the daughter of Jarius, a synagogue ruler	Mk. 5:22-42 Mt. 9:18-24 Lk. 8:41-55	Jesus took the girl by the hand and said, "Little girl, I say to you, get up!" (Mk.5:41)
Gynecologic bleeding in a woman for twelve years, unresponsive to treatment by many doctors.	Mk. 5:25-34 Mt. 9:20-22 Lk. 8:43-48	Jesus became aware that someone touched his cloak, and said, "I know that power has gone out from me." The woman told Jesus that she had touched him and that her bleeding had stopped. Jesus said, "Daughter, your faith has healed you. Go in peace and be freed from your suffering." (Mk. 5:34)
Sicknesses in people placed in the marketplaces.	Mk. 6:55-56 Mt. 14:35-36	All who touched Jesus were healed.

---

[*] The spiritual healing events are listed in order first as reported in the Gospel of Mark, and then in the Gospels of Matthew, Luke, and John.

Spiritual Healing by Jesus (cont'd)

Illnesses Healed	Sources	How Jesus Healed
Evil spirit possessing the daughter of a Canaanite woman. (daughter of a Syrophoenician woman in Mk.).	Mk. 7:25-30 Mt. 15:22-28	After the woman begged Jesus to drive the demon out of her daughter, and spoke to him on faith, he said, "Woman, you have great faith! Your request is granted." (Mt. 15:28)
Deafness and a speech impediment in a man in the region of the Decapolis.	Mk. 7:32-35	Jesus put his fingers into the man's ears, spit and touched the man's tongue, sighed deeply and said, "Be opened." (Mk. 7:34)
Blindness in a man.	Mk. 8:22-26	Jesus spit and put his hands on the man's eyes, and the man's sight was partially restored. Jesus then put his hands on the man's eyes again, and the man's sight was fully restored.
Evil spirit possessing a boy, causing muteness and convulsions, which Jesus' disciples were unable to exorcise.	Mk. 9:17-29 Mt. 7:14-20 Lk. 9:38-42	Jesus said to the evil spirit, "I command you, come out of him and never enter him again." (Mk. 9:25)
Blindness in Bartimaeus (blind beggar in Luke).	Mk. 10:46-52 Lk. 18:35-43	Jesus said to Bartimaeus, who was blind, "Receive your sight; your faith has healed you." (Lk. 18:42)
Various diseases, and demonic possessions, epilepsy and paralyses in people in the region of Galilee.	Mt. 4:23-25 Lk. 6:17-20	Not described.
Paralysis in a centurion's servant.	Mt. 8:5-13	Jesus told the centurion that his servant would be healed. Jesus then said to his followers that he had not found anyone in Israel "with such great faith" as the centurion. (Mt. 8:10)
Blindness in two men.	Mt. 9:27-30	Jesus touched the men's eyes and said, "According to your faith it will be done to you." (Mt. 9:29)
Demon possessing a man, who was mute.	Mt. 9:32-33	Not described.
Disease and sickness in all the towns and villages.	Mt. 9:35-37	Jesus "had compassion" on the crowds. How he healed was not described.
Demon possessing a man, who was blind and mute.	Mt. 12:22 Lk. 11:14	Not described.
Sickness in the crowds.	Mt. 14:14 Lk. 9:11 Jn. 6:2	Jesus "had compassion" when he saw a large crowd on the shore. How he healed was not described.
Lameness, blindness, muteness and many other sicknesses in people brought by the crowds.	Mt. 15:30-31	Not described.
Sickness in large crowds.	Mt. 19:2	Not described.
Blindness in two men.	Mt. 20:30-34	Jesus "had compassion" on the men, and touched their eyes. (Mt. 30:34)

Spiritual Healing by Jesus (cont'd)

Illnesses Healed	Sources	How Jesus Healed
Blindness and lameness in people at the temple.	Mt. 21:14	Not described.
Sicknesses in crowds of people.	Lk: 5:15	Not described.
Death of the son of a widow in Nain.	Lk: 7:11-15	When Jesus first saw the widow, "his heart went out to her and he said, 'Don't cry.' " (Lk. 7:13). He touched the coffin and said, "Young man, I say to you, get up!" (7:14).
Evil spirit possessions of and diseases in many women, including Mary Magdalene.	Lk. 8:2	Not described.
A spirit possessing a woman and crippling her, for eighteen years.	Lk. 13:10-14	Jesus said to the woman, "Woman, you are set free from your infirmity." (Lk. 13:12) Then he placed his hands on her.
Dropsy in a man.	Lk. 14:2-4	Jesus took hold of the man.
Leprosy in ten men.	Lk. 17:12-19	Jesus told the men to show themselves to priests, and as they went they were healed. Jesus said to the only man who returned to thank him for being healed, "your faith has made you well." (Lk. 17:19)
Severed ear of the high priest's slave.	Lk. 22:50-51	Jesus touched the man's ear.
Fever in the son of a royal official.	Jn. 4:46-53	Jesus said to the royal official, "You may go. Your son will live." (Jn. 4:50)
Disabling condition of thirty-eight years, in a man at the pool of Bethesda.	Jn. 5:2-15	Jesus said to the man, "Get up! Pick up your mat and walk." (Jn. 5:8) When Jesus saw the man later at the temple, he said to him, "Stop sinning or something worse may happen to you." (5:14)
Blindness in a man from birth.	Jn.9:1-7	Jesus used his saliva to make mud, which he put on the man's eyes and said to the man "Go, wash in the Pool of Siloam." (Jn. 9:7)
Death of Lazarus following an illness.	Jn. 11:1-44	When Jesus heard of Lazarus' death, he was "deeply moved in spirit and troubled," and "wept." (Jn. 11:33, 35). Jesus called to Lazarus in the tomb, "Lazarus, come out!" (11:43).

Appendix B

Spiritual Healing in the Book of Acts

Sources	What Occurred
3:1-10	Peter and John encountered a man who had been crippled from birth, begging at the temple gate. Peter ordered the man to look at them, and said, "In the name of Jesus Christ of Nazareth, walk." (3:6) When Peter helped the man to his feet, "instantly the man's feet and ankles became strong." (3:7)
5:15	The sick were laid on beds and mats in the streets "so that at least Peter's shadow might fall on some of them as he passed by."
5:16	Those who were sick and tormented by evil spirits were brought from towns around Jerusalem, and "all of them were healed" by the apostles.
8:6-7	During Philip's ministry in Samaria "With shrieks, evil spirits came out of many, and many paralytics and cripples were healed." (8:7)
9:17	Ananias, a disciple, placed his hands on Saul (later called the apostle Paul) and cured him of the blindness that had suddenly occurred during his vision of Jesus on the road to Damascus.
9:32-34	In Lydda Peter encountered Aeneas, a paralyzed man who had been bedridden for eight years. Peter said to him "Jesus Christ heals you. Get up and take care of your mat. Immediately Aeneas got up." (9:34)
9:36-41	In Joppa a disciple named Tabitha died and Peter was urged to come to her. He "got down on his knees and prayed. Turning toward the dead woman, he said 'Tabitha, get up.' She opened her eyes, and seeing Peter she sat up." (9:40)
14:8	In Lystra a man who was crippled in his feet and lame from birth was healed by Paul when he recognized the man's faith and then said to him, "Stand up on your feet!"
16:16-18	Paul was being followed by a slave girl who had a spirit that enabled her to predict the future. He said, " 'In the name of Jesus Christ I command you to come out of her!' At that moment the spirit left her." (16:18)
19:12	Handkerchiefs and aprons that had touched Paul "were taken to the sick, and their illnesses were cured and the evil spirits left them."
20:8-10	In Troas a young man named Eutychus was seated on a window ledge, listening to Paul talk on into the evening, when he went into a deep sleep, fell out of the window to the ground three stories below, and died. Paul "threw himself on the young man and put his arms around him," (20:10) and the man revived.
28:7-8	Paul healed Publius, the father of the chief official of the island of Malta, who was bedridden by fever and dysentery. Paul "went in to see him and, after prayer, placed his hands upon him and healed him." (28:8)
28:9	After Paul healed Publius, he healed the rest of the sick people on Malta.

Appendix C

Example of a Healing Service

HEALING SERVICE

(Where)

(When)

Into God's Presence   Canon in D   Pachelbel

Words of Inspiration *(Leader or Reader)*

> Good people,
> Most royal greening verdancy,
> Rooted in the sun,
> You shine with radiant light.
> In this circle of earthly existence
> You shine so finely,
> It surpasses understanding.
> God hugs you.
> You are encircled by the arms
> of the mystery of God.

Hildegard of Bingen

Welcome *(Leader)*

> A most warm welcome to everyone who has come to our healing service. With faith in God's love for us and in our love for God and each other, we have come together to pray for spiritual healing. First we will fully open our minds and spirits to God. Then those who desire spiritual healing of themselves or persons who are not here will be invited to come forward, so that we may lay our hands upon them and pray for healing. The laying on of hands is an ancient, universal, religious practice for channeling

the healing energy of the Holy Spirit to those who desire healing of themselves or others.

I now invite you to welcome those around you in the spirit of love.

Scripture *(Leader or Reader)*

Jesus of Nazareth was a remarkable spiritual healer, and he commissioned his disciples to go out into the world to heal, as well as to teach and preach, as he did. Spiritual healing has continued in the Church to this day. In the following readings from the Gospels of Matthew and John, Jesus heals people who are able and unable to come to him, as we will ask God to do in this healing service.

When he [Jesus] came down from the mountainside, large crowds followed him. A man with leprosy came and knelt before him and said, "Lord, if you are willing, you can make me clean." Jesus reached out his hand and touched the man. "I am willing," he said. "Be clean!" Immediately he was cured of his leprosy. *(Matthew 8:1-3)*

Once more he [Jesus] visited Cana in Galilee, where he had turned the water into wine. And there was a certain royal official whose son lay sick at Capernaum. When this man heard that Jesus had arrived in Galilee from Judea, he went to him and begged him to come and heal his son, who was close to death. "Unless you people see miraculous signs and wonders," Jesus said, "you will never believe." The royal official said, "Sir, come down before my child dies." Jesus replied, "You may go. Your son will live." The man took Jesus at his word and departed. While he was still on the way, his servants met him with the news that his boy was living. When he inquired as to the time when his son got better, they said to him, "The fever left him yesterday at the seventh hour." Then the father realized that this was the exact time at which Jesus said to him, "Your son will live." So he and all of his household believed. *(John 4:46-53)*

Song (All)

Breathe on me, Breath of God,
fill me with life anew,
that I may love the way you love,
and do what you would do.

Breathe on me Breath of God,
stir in me one desire:
That every earthly part of me
may glow with earthly fire.

Message *(Leader)*

Jesus said, "I tell you the truth, if anyone says to this mountain, 'Go, throw yourself into the sea,' and does not doubt in his heart but believes that what he says will happen, it will be done for him. Therefore I tell you, whatever you ask for in prayer, believe that you have received it, and it will be yours." (Mark 11:23-24.)

In these verses from the Gospel of Mark, Jesus is reassuring his disciples about the power of prayer, as he gives them the knowledge and experience necessary to carry on his ministry, including spiritual healing, when he is no longer with them. We might wonder: Why did Jesus have to give the disciples this reassurance when, according to the Gospels, he had already empowered them for spiritual healing and sent them out to heal with remarkable success? An appropriate answer to this question might be that Jesus' disciples, being ordinary people like us, were prone to need reassurance of God's love and support while being trained for such a challenging ministry.

Do we need to have at least some reassurance that spiritual healing still occurs? If so, we can look back at the long history of spiritual healing and even listen to persons who have experienced it. But whether or not we need this reassurance, Jesus is telling us that when we really believe that prayer for healing works, it will!

Soon we will pray to God for the healing of those who are with us and for those who are not with us. Although the prayer that we use during the laying on of hands asks for healing "according to God's will," the person for whom we are praying may also wish that we pray for a specific healing.

Spiritual healing occurs when we humbly, sincerely, and trustingly ask God for help in healing our own or another person's illness. When we experience healing, we may find ourselves regaining physical, mental, emotional, and spiritual strength, being able to live with an illness and its effects, coming closer to God and loved ones, and feeling peace at the end of life. And, for some, healing can be so great that the illness is actually cured.

We may believe that God punishes us for our sins by making us ill. However, Jesus would tell us that God does not punish us with illness, but out of unconditional love for us desires that we be whole in body, mind and spirit. Therefore, we should release the thought of illness being God's punishment from our minds.

The following guided meditation will also help us get into a spiritually healthy attitude for communicating freely with God for spiritual healing, by calming our minds and clearing them of troublesome thoughts and emotions.

Guided Meditation *(Leader or Reader)*

Let us prepare ourselves for a guided meditation by relaxing comfortably in our chairs, with our hands apart on our laps and our feet flat on the floor. Now close your eyes, and breathe slowly and deeply three times, in through your nose and out through your mouth. *(Accompany the breathing exercise with "in through your nose and out through your mouth.")*

Imagine that you are alone on a beach on a warm summer day, walking barefoot over a stretch of sand kept moist by small waves washing up on the shore. To your right the dark blue water stretches to the horizon, where it blends with the cloudless blue sky. And to your left small dunes of fine rippled sand are capped by tall grass swaying in the gentle breeze. *(Pause)*

You stop and look about you at the water, sky and sand, and momentarily experience a sense of being at peace. *(Pause)* You ask yourself, "Why can't I feel this way all the time? *(Pause)* Almost immediately an inner voice replies: "Because your mind is cluttered with so many troublesome thoughts and emotions." *(Pause)* Then the voice tells you, "Go to the water's edge and write a thought or emotion that is bothering you in the moist sand, and let a wave come and wash it away." *(Pause)*

You pick up a small, smooth stick, and kneel at the water's edge. As a wave recedes, you write in the sand, "fear," which is washed away by the next wave. *(Pause)* Then you write, "guilt," which is washed away by the next wave. *(Pause)* *(Repeat separately for anger, resentment, remorse, jealousy, doubt, despair, sorrow, etc.) (Pause)*

When you have nothing more to write in the sand and be washed away, you realize that you are again experiencing the sense of being at peace, and that this time it does not go away. You continue walking along the beach, enjoying its beauty. *(Pause)*

You may open your eyes when you wish.

Song (All)

Come forth, O Love divine,
seek now this soul of mine,
and visit it with your own ardor glowing;
O Comforter, draw near,
within my heart appear,
and kindle it, your holy flame bestowing.

And so the yearning strong
with which the soul; will long,
shall far out-pass the power of human telling;
For none can guess its grace,
till love create a place
wherein the Holy Spirit makes a dwelling.

A Prayer for Healing (All)

All-powerful God, source of all healing, make those for whom we pray for healing fully aware of your presence with them. Open their eyes that they may see you; open their ears that they hear you; open their hearts that they may know your love. Cast the light of your Spirit upon them, so that they may be healed in body, mind, and spirit.

The Lord's Prayer (All)

Our Father, who art in heaven, hallowed be thy name. Thy kingdom come. Thy will be done on earth as it is in heaven. Give us this day our daily bread. And forgive us our trespasses, as we

forgive those who trespass against us. And lead us not into temptation, but deliver us from evil. For thine is the kingdom, and the power, and the glory, for ever and ever. Amen.

The Laying on of Hands

(Those who do not participate in the laying on of hands are asked to join in prayer.)

<u>With hands being laid upon a person who desires his or her own healing</u>

(All) **As God loves us, we lay our hands upon you to help you receive divine healing energy. With faith in God and in the name of Jesus Christ, we pray for your healing according to God's will.**

(Additional prayers by individuals are invited.)

<u>With hands being laid upon a person who desires healing of another</u>

(All) **As God loves us, we lay our hands upon you to help you receive and send divine healing energy to _____. With faith in God and in the name of Jesus Christ, we pray for his/her healing according to God's will.**

(Additional prayers by individuals are invited.)

Prayer of Thankfulness (All)

God of all love, we are deeply thankful that you have heard our prayers and have blessed us with healing of body, mind and spirit. We humbly ask that you will continue to assist back to health those for whom we have prayed.

Parting Song (All, holding hands, standing if able)

Alleluia, alleluia, alleluia, alleluia,
Alleluia, alleluia, alleluia, alleluia.

Benediction *(Leader)*

As we leave this place we commend ourselves to
God's everlasting care, ever mindful of God's healing
presence in our lives.

Appendix D

Example of a Twenty-Minute Gathering for Spiritual Healing

TWENTY-MINUTE GATHERING FOR SPIRITUAL HEALING

Words of Inspiration *(Leader or Reader)*

> I lift my eyes up to the hills -
>   where does my help come from?
> My help comes from the LORD,
>   the Maker of heaven and earth.
>
> He will not let your foot slip -
>   he who watches over you will not slumber;
>
> The LORD watches over you -
>   the LORD is your shade at your right hand;
> the sun will not harm you by day,
>   nor the moon by night.
>
> The LORD will keep you from all harm -
>   he will watch over your life;
> the LORD will watch over your coming and going
>   both now and forevermore.

Psalm 121:1-3, 5-8

or

> Jesus said, "I tell you the truth, if anyone says to this mountain, 'Go, throw yourself into the sea,' and does not doubt in his heart but believes that what he says will happen, it will be done for him. Therefore, I tell you, whatever you ask for in prayer, believe that you have received it, and it will be yours.

Mark 11:23-24

or

You could make this place alive,
divine, infused with inner light.
You can take your shy, secret hopes
and construct them into what they might.

The place can be anywhere.
The only source is within you.
All that you see was once a dream.
Dream again today and that you do become.

Barry Harris

or

May we learn to open in love
so all the doors and windows
of our bodies swing wide
on their rusty hinges.

May we learn to give ourselves with both hands,
to lift each other on our shoulders,
to carry one another along.

May holiness move in us
so we may pay attention to its small voice
and honor its light in each other.

Dawna Markova

Welcome *(Leader)*

A most warm welcome to everyone who has come to
our healing service. With faith in God's love for us
and in our love for God and each other, we have
come together to pray for spiritual healing. First we
will fully open our minds and spirits to God. Then
those who desire spiritual healing of themselves or
persons who are not here will be invited to come
forwards, so that we may lay our hands upon them
and pray for healing. The laying on of hands is an

ancient, universal, religious practice for channeling the healing energy of the Holy Spirit to those who desire healing of themselves or others.

Guided Meditation *(Leader or Reader)*

Prayer for Healing *(Leader)*

<u>With hands being laid upon a person who desires his or her own healing</u>

(Leader) As God loves us, we lay our hands upon you to help you receive divine healing energy. With faith in God, we pray for your healing according to God's will.

(The leader may say additional prayers and should invite others to pray.)

<u>With hands being laid upon a person who desires healing of another</u>

(Leader) As God loves us, we lay our hands upon you to help you receive and send divine healing energy to _____. With faith in God, we pray for his/her healing according to God's will.

(The leader may say additional prayers and should invite others to pray.)

Prayer of Thankfulness *(Leader or Reader)*

Loving God, we are deeply thankful that you have listened to our prayers for healing and have provided the healing energy of your Spirit to those for whom we have prayed. We humbly ask that you continue to send them your gift of healing.

or

91

We thank you, God, for blessing all of us with the healing energy of your Spirit. We ask that you help us to be constantly mindful of your unconditional love for us, and your desire that we be whole in body, mind and spirit.

Notes

Part I: Introduction

1. The Holy Bible, New International Version (Grand Rapids, MI: Zondervan Bible Publishers, 1996). Copyright © 1996 by Zondervan Corporation. Copyright © 1973, 1978, 1984 by International Bible Society.

Part II: How Can We Connect for Spiritual Healing?

1. Erwin H. Ackerknecht, *A Short History of Medicine,* (Baltimore: The John Hopkins University Press, 1982), 20.
2. Magner, *A History of Medicine,* (New York: Marcel Dekker, Inc., 1992), 29.
3. Ibid., 26.
4. Ackerknecht, *A Short History of Medicine,* 25.
5. Magner, *A History of Medicine,* 29-31.
6. Ibid., 26.
7. Ibid., 26.
8. Ackerknecht, *A Short History of Medicine,* 27-28.
9. Magner, *A History of Medicine,* 19.
10. Ackerknecht, *A Short History of Medicine,* 28.
11. Magner, *A History of Medicine,* 19.
12. Ackerknecht, *A Short History of Medicine,* 29.
13. Morton Kelsey, *Healing and Christianity: A Classic Study* (Minneapolis, MN: Augsburg Fortress, 1995), 37.
14. Ackerknecht, *A Short History of Medicine,* 55-63.
15. Magner, *A History of Medicine,* 68.
16. Ackerknecht, *A Short History of Medicine,* 48.
17. Magner, *A History of Medicine,* 74-75.
18. Kenneth L. Bakken, *The Journey into God: Healing and the Christian Faith* (Minneapolis, MN: Augsburg Fortress, 2000), 12; Kelsey, *Healing and Christianity,* 26-27.
19. Ibid., 27.
20. In Moses' song to the whole assembly of Israel, God said, "See now that I myself am He! There is no God besides me. I put to death and bring to life, I have wounded and I will heal, and no one can deliver out of my hand." (Deut. 32:39) See also Ex. 4:11, Isa. 45:7 and Amos 3:6.

21. After making water from a spring drinkable for the Jews in the wilderness, God made a decree and a law and then tested them, saying "if you listen carefully to the voice of the LORD your God and do what is right in God's eyes, if you pay attention to his commands and keep all his decrees, I will not bring on you any of the diseases I brought on the Egyptians, for I am the LORD who heals you." (Ex. 15:26) See also Lev. 16:26, 25, Deut. 28:27-29 and Prov. 3:7-8.

22. In giving Moses the Ten Commandments, God said, "the LORD ... punishes the children and their children for the sin of the fathers to the third and fourth generation." (Ex. 33:7) See also Ex. 20:5.

23. "In those days *[referring to when the Jews would return to Jerusalem from their exile in Babylon]* people will no longer say, 'The fathers have eaten sour grapes, and the children's teeth are set on edge.' Instead, everyone will die for his own sin: whoever eats sour grapes - his own teeth will be set on edge." (Jer. 31:28, 29) See also Ezek. 18:2-3.

24. "O LORD, do not rebuke me in your anger or discipline me in your wrath. Be merciful to me, LORD, for I am faint; O LORD, heal me, for my bones are in agony" (Ps. 6:1-2) and "I said, 'O LORD, have mercy on me; heal me, for I have sinned against you.'" (41:1) See also Ps. 38:1-3; 119:65-72.

25. In this ancient folktale God allows Satan (functions as an "adversary" or "accuser" in the Old Testament) to test Job, a saintly man, with suffering to prove to God that Job will "fear God for nothing." (Job 1:9) Job repeatedly professes that he is innocent of any wrongdoing, and so his suffering is undeserved, while maintaining his faith in God.

26. James L. Crenshaw, *The HarperCollins Study Bible: New Revised Standard Version* (New York: HarperCollins Publishers, 1993), 751.

27. Num. 11:18-20, 31-33; 16:41-50.

28. See discussion of leprosy under "Spiritual Healing in New Testament Times."

29. Num. 12:1, 5-10.

30. 2 Sam. 24:1, 15.

31. Gen. 12:10-15, 17. A similar story of Abraham, Sarah and King Abimelech is told in Gen. 20:1-3, 14-18.

32. 2 Kings 5:25-27.

33. John A. Sanford, *Healing Body and Soul: The Meaning of Illness in the New Testament and in Psychotherapy* (Louisville, KY: Westminster John Knox Press, 1992), 13-14.

34. See Lev. 11-16.

35. Barry L. Bandstra, *Reading the Old Testament: An Introduction to the Hebrew Bible* (New York: Wadsworth, 1995), 150; Howard

Clark Key, *Medicine, Miracle and Magic in New Testament Times* (New York: Cambridge University Press, 1986), 11.

36. 2 Chr. 16:11-12; Jer. 8:22-9:6; Jer. 33:12-13.
37. Kelsey, *Healing and Christianity*, 31.
38. Sir. 38:1-15. Sirach was written about 190 B.C.E. (Kelsey, *Healing and Christianity*, 31). The shift in attitude towards physicians may have been influenced by exposure of the Jews to Greek medicine. (Key, *Medicine, Miracle and Magic in New Testament Times*, 20-21; see also below).
39. Julius Preuss, *Biblical and Talmudic Medicine*, translated from the German and edited by Fred Rosner (Northvale, NJ: Jason Aronson Inc., 1993), 28.
40. Ibid.
41. "Then Abraham prayed to God, and God healed Abimelech, his wife and his slave girls so that they could have children again." (Gen. 20:17)
42. "Then the king said to the man of God, 'intercede with the LORD your God and pray for me that my hand may be restored.' So the man of God interceded with the LORD, and the king's hand was restored and became as it was before." (1Kings 13:6)
43. "He took him from her arms, carried him to the upper room where he was staying, and laid him on his bed. ... Then he stretched himself out on the boy three times and cried to the LORD, 'O LORD my God, let this boy's life return to him!' The LORD heard Elijah's cry, and the boy's life returned to him, and he lived." (1 Kings 17:19, 21-22)
44. 2 Kings 4:32-35.
45. "Now Naaman was commander of the army of the king of Aram. ... He was a valiant soldier, but he had leprosy. ... Elisha sent a messenger *[when Naaman came to Elisha's house]* to say to him, 'Go, wash yourself seven times in the Jordan, and your flesh will be restored and you will be cleansed.' ... So he went down and dipped himself in the Jordan seven times, as the man of God had told him, and his flesh was restored and became clean like that of a young boy." (2 Kings 5:1, 10, 14)
46. 2 Kings 20:1-11.
47. "Be strong, do not fear; your God will come, he will come with a vengeance; with divine retribution he will come to save you. Then the eyes of the blind will be opened and the ears of the deaf unstopped. Then will the lame leap like a deer and the mute tongue shout for joy," (Isa. 35:4-6) and "but for you who revere my name, the sun of righteousness will rise with healing in its wings." (Mal. 4:2)
48. Isa. 53:11.

49. "Surely he took up our infirmities and carried our sorrows, yet we considered him stricken by God, smitten by him, and afflicted. But he was pierced for our transgressions, he was crushed for our iniquities; the punishment that brought us peace was upon him, and by his wounds we are healed." (Isa. 53:4)

50. Mt. 11:5; Lk. 7:22.

51. Kelsey, *Healing and Christianity*, 42.

52. For example, the multiple demons that possessed the man in the region of the Gerasenes appears to have been interpreted metaphorically as Roman legions, and Jesus' exorcism of these unclean spirits into pigs, which were considered unclean animals, would seem appropriate.

53. Jewish oral tradition provided the gospel writers with reasonably accurate information. See John Dominic Crossan, *The Birth of Christianity: Discovering What Happened in the Years Immediately After the Execution of Jesus* (San Francisco: HarperSanFrancisco, 1998) and N. T. Wright, "The Crux of Faith," in Marcus T. Borg and N. T. Wright, *The Meaning of Jesus: Two Visions* (San Francisco: HarperSanFrancisco, 1999), 94-95.

54. Max Sussman, "Sickness and Disease," in *The Anchor Bible Dictionary, Volume 6* (New York: Doubleday, 1992), 10.

55. Ibid.

56. Ibid.; Stevan L. Davies, *Jesus the Healer: Possession, Trance, and the Origin of Christianity* (New York: Continuum, 1995), 68.

57. Preuss, *Biblical and Talmudic Medicine,* 139-140.

58. God punished King Saul for disobeying a divine order by sending an evil spirit to possess and torment him. The spirit would leave Saul and he would feel better when David played the lyre for him. (1 Sam. 15:22-23; 16:14-15, 23). See also the apocryphal book of Tobit:6:8, 14; 8:2-3.

59. Tom Harpur, *The Uncommon Touch: An Investigation of Spiritual Healing* (Toronto, Ontario: McClelland & Stewart Inc., 1994), 63.

60. Davies, *Jesus the Healer*, 85-86; Key, *Medicine, Miracle and Magic in New Testament Times,* 78-79; Sanford, *Healing Body and Soul,* 20.

61. See Davies, *Jesus the Healer*; Edith Fiore, *The Unquiet Dead: A Psychologist Treats Spirit Possession* (Garden City, NY: Doubleday & Company, Inc., 1987); Samuel Sagan, *Entity Possession: Freeing the Energy Body of Negative Influences* (Rochester, VT: Destiny Books, 1997); and Francis MacNutt, *Deliverance from Evil Spirits: A Practical Manual* (Grand Rapids, MI: Chosen Books, 1995).

62. Consideration of the existence of actual demons, or spirits beholden to Satan, is beyond the scope of this book.

63. Mt. 14:14; Mk. 1:41; Lk. 9:11, and Mt. 20:34; Jn 6:2.

64. Kelsey, *Healing and Christianity,* 51.

65. Jn. 9:2.

66. Ibid., 55.

67. Mt. 8:24; Mk 4:38; Lk. 8:23, and Mt. 14:23; Mk. 6:46; Lk. 6:12.

68. Key, *Medicine, Miracle and Magic in New Testament Times,* 78.

69. For example, the man with leprosy. (Mt. 8:2-3; Mk. 1:40-42; Lk. 5:12-13)

70. For example, the Syrophoenician woman's daughter (Mt. 15:22-28; Mk. 7:25-30).

71. For example, the man with the withered hand. (Mt. 12:9-13; Mk. 3:1-5; Lk. 6:6-10)

72. Mk. 5:30; Lk. 8:46.

73. Preuss, *Biblical and Talmudic Medicine,* 277.

74. An example of Jesus healing at a distance is his healing of the royal official's son. (Jn. 4:43-53) An example of Jesus healing in direct contact is his healing of deafness and a speech impediment in a man in the region of the Decapolis. (Mk. 7:32-35)

75. Mk. 9:28-29.

76. Mt. 21:22; Mk. 11:24; Jn. 14:13-14; 15:7; 16:23.

77. Mt. 9:2; Mk. 2:5; Lk. 5:20.

78. Mt. 15:28.

79. Mt. 9:27.

80. Mt. 9:22; Mk. 5:34; Lk. 8:48.

81. Mk. 10:52; Lk. 18:42.

82. Lk. 17:12.

83. Mt. 8:10.

84. Kelsey, *Healing and Christianity,* 68-69.

85. "As he *[Jesus]* went along, he saw a man blind from birth. His disciples asked him, 'Rabbi, who sinned, this man or his parents, that he was born blind?' 'Neither this man nor his parents sinned', said Jesus." (Jn. 9:1-2)

86. "Since they could not get him *[a paralyzed man]* to Jesus because of the crowd, they made an opening in the roof above Jesus and, after digging through it, lowered the mat the paralyzed man was lying on. When Jesus saw their faith, he said to the paralytic, 'Son, your sins are forgiven.'" (Mk. 2:4-5)

87. "Now there is in Jerusalem near the Sheep Gate a pool, which in Aramaic is called Bethesda ... Here a great number of people used to lie – the blind, the lame, the paralyzed. One who was there had been an invalid for thirty-eight years. When Jesus saw him there and learned that he had been in this condition for a long time, he asked him, 'Do you want to get well?' 'Sir,' the invalid replied, 'I have no one to help me into the pool when the water is stirred. While I'm trying to get in, someone else goes down ahead of me.' Then Jesus said to him, 'Get up! Pick up your mat and walk.' At

once the man was cured; he picked up his mat and walked. ... Later Jesus found him in the temple and said to him, 'See, you are well again. Stop sinning or something worse may happen to you.'" (Jn. 5:2-9, 14)

88. Pheme Perkins, "The Gospel of Mark," in *The New Interpreter's Bible, Volume VIII* (Nashville, TN: Abington Press, 1995), 550.

89. Sanford, *Healing Body and Soul*, 26-29.

90. The hint of an answer comes from the Jesus' name, Yeshua, in Hebrew, which means "Yahweh is healing." (Bakken, *The Journey into God,* 19.)

91. Bakken, *The Journey into God,* 18-19; Davies, *Jesus the Healer*, 93; Kelsey, *Healing and Christianity,* 49, 70-73; John Wimber and Kevin Springer, *Power Healing* (New York: HarperCollins, 1987), 12-13, 15-16.

92. Mt. 10:1, 5-11; Mk. 6:7, 12-13; Lk. 9:1-2, 6.

93. Lk. 10:1, 9.

94. Acts 2:43; 5:12; 6:8; 8:13; 14:3; 15:12.

95. Acts 9:36-41.

96. Acts 28:8.

97. Acts 14:8.

98. Acts 5:1-10.

99. Acts 13:6-12.

100. 1 Cor. 11:27-33.

101. 2 Cor. 12:7-10.

102. Prov. 3:11-12.

103. Heb 12:5-6.

104. 1 Cor. 12:1-11.

105. 1 Cor. 12:8, 9.

106. 1 Cor. 12:4-6.

107. Anointing for healing is mentioned in the Gospels. When Jesus first sent his twelve disciples out for ministry, they "anointed many sick people and healed them." (Mk. 6:13)

108. "I tell you the truth, anyone who has faith in me will do what I have been doing. He will do even greater things than these, because I am going to the Father, so that the Son may bring glory to the Father. You may ask me for anything in my name, and I will do it." (Jn.14:12)

109. Neil Douglas-Klotz, *Prayers of the Cosmos: Meditations on the Aramaic Words of Jesus* (San Francisco: HarperSanFrancisco, 1990), 86-88; Roth with Ochiogrosso, *The Healing Path of Prayer*, 72.

110. Kelsey, *Healing and Christianity,* 104.

111. Abigail Rian Evans, *The Healing Church: Practical Programs for Healing Ministries* (Cleveland, OH: United Church Press, 1999), 6.

112. Kelsey, *Healing and Christianity,* 108-121, 126-140, 145-156, 132.

113. Ibid., 121-122, 141.
114. Ibid., 141-142.
115. Ibid.
116. Ibid.
117. Bakken, *The Journey into God*, 32; Kelsey, *Healing and Christianity*, 92.
118. Bakken, *The Journey into God*, 31.
119. Kelsey, *Healing and Christianity*, 154-155.
120. Ibid., 169.
121. This plague killed one-third of the European population. In 1348 Pope Nicholas V declared it a punishment from God for the sins of humanity. See Bakken, *The Journey into God*, 34-35 and Kelsey, *Healing and Christianity*, 166-167.
122. International Commission on English in the Liturgy, *Pastoral Care of the Sick: Rites of Anointing and Viaticum* (New York: Roman Catholic Book Publishing, 1983), 15.
123. Ibid., 15.
124. Ibid., 15-16.
125. Kelsey, *Healing and Christianity*, 165.
126. Ibid., 168.
127. Ibid., 170-171.
128. Bakken, *The Journey into God*, 34.
129. Ibid., 35-36.
130. Kelsey, *Healing and Christianity*, 173.
131. Ibid., 183.
132. Ibid., 174.
133. Ibid. 12-13, 174.
134. Kelsey, *Healing and Christianity*, 136, 139.
135. Ibid., 177-178.
136. Ibid., 180.
137. Ruth Cranston, *The Miracle of Lourdes: Updated and Expanded Edition by the Medical Bureau of Lourdes* (New York: Image Books, 1988); Frederic Flach, *Faith, Healing, and Miracles* (New York: Hatherleigh Press, 2000), 31-42.
138. Kelsey, *Healing and Christianity*, 149-150, 179-184.
139. See Friedrich Zuendel, *The Awakening: One Man's Battle With Darkness* (Farmington, PA: Plough Publishing House, 2000).
140. David Edwin Harrell, Jr., *All Things are Possible: The Healing and Charismatic Revivals in Modern America* (Bloomington, IN: Indiana University Press, 1975), 190-191.
141. Ibid., 27-42.
142. Ibid., 41-52.
143. Joel S. Goldsmith, *The Art of Spiritual Healing* (San Francisco: HarperSanFrancisco, 1959).

144. Agnes Sanford, *The Healing Light* (New York: Ballantyne Books, 1972).
145. Francis MacNutt, *Healing* (Notre Dame, IN: Ave Maria Press, 1999). See also Harrell, *All Things Are Possible*, 228.
146. Ron Roth with Peter Occhiogrosso, *The Healing Path of Prayer: A Modern Mystic's Guide to Spiritual Power* (New York: Three Rivers Press, 1997).

Part III: Connecting in a Healing Service

1. 1 Cor. 12:4-6, 9.
2. Herbert Benson, *Timeless Healing: The Power and Biology of Belief* (New York: Fireside, 1996), 195-199.
3. Gregg Braden, *The God Code: The Secret of our Past, the Promise of Our Future*, (Carlsbad, CA: Hay House, Inc., 2004), 115-143.
4. Ibid., 155. See also L. Robert Keck, *Healing as a Sacred Path: A Story of Personal Medical and Spiritual Transformation* (West Chester, PA: Chrysalis Books, 2002), 272-273 and Paul Tillich, *Theology of Culture* (New York: Oxford University Press, 1959), 7-9.
5. "Now faith is being sure of what we hope for and certain of what we do not see." (Heb. 11:1)
6. Candace B. Pert, *Molecules of Emotion: The Science of Mind-Body Medicine* (New York: Touchstone, 1997).
7. Larry Dossey, *Reinventing Medicine: Beyond Mind-Body to a New Era of Healing* (San Francisco: HarperSanFrancisco, 1999), 21-24.
8. Benson, *Timeless Healing*, 20-21; Dossey, R*einventing Medicine,* 8, 22, 164-165; Thomas A. Droege, *The Faith Factor in Healing* (Philadelphia: Trinity Press International, 1991), 7-12.
9. A placebo is a harmless substance or procedure.
10. Referring here to a unified system of beliefs and practices relating to the sacred, within a community.
11. Referring here to an optimal state of physical, mental, and emotional wellbeing.
12. Jeff Levin, God, *Faith and Health: Exploring the Spirituality-Healing Connection* (New York; John Wiley & Sons, Inc., 2001), 31-32, 89.
13. Harold G. Koenig, *Is Religion Good for Your Health? The Effects of Religion on Physical and Mental Health* (New York: Haworth Pastoral Press, 1997), 78-82. See also Levin*, God, Faith and Health,* 19-149.
14. Ibid., 94; Droege, *The Faith Factor in Healing*, 26.

15. MacNutt, *Healing*, 94-95; Tilda Norberg and Robert D. Webber, *Stretch Out Your Hand: Exploring Healing Prayer* (Nashville, TN: Upper Room Books, 1998), 43.
16. MacNutt, *Healing*, 95-97.
17. Lk. 15:11-31.
18. Lk. 15:20.
19. Epperly, *God's Touch*, 17; MacNutt, *Healing*, 123.
20. Russell Targ and Jane Katra, *Miracles of the Mind: Exploring Nonlocal Consciousness and Spiritual Healing* (Novato, CA: New World Library, 1999), 260; Dossey, *Reinventing Medicine*, 90.
21. Flach, *Faith, Healing, and Miracles*, 82; Sanford, *Healing Body and Soul*, 20, 22, 70.
22. Larry Dossey, *Healing Words: The Power of Prayer and the Practice of Medicine* (San Francisco: HarperSanFrancisco, 1993), 169-195; Daniel J. Benor, *Spiritual Healing: Scientific Validation of a Healing Revolution, Healing Research Volume I* (Southfield, MI: Vision Publications, 2001).
23. According to this concept, the nonlocal mind is unbounded and infinite in space and time, and can produce effects in others. (Dossey, *Healing Words*, 41) See also Benor, *Spiritual Healing*, 164-168, 181-185; Dossey, *Reinventing Medicine*, 32-84; Amit Goswami, *Physics of the Soul: The Quantum Book of Living, Dying, Reincarnation, and Immortality* (Charlottesville, VA: Hampton Roads Publishing Company, 2001), 14-15; and Targ and Katra, *Miracles of the Mind*, 18, 27, 142-143, 232.
24. Dossey, *Healing Words*, 83-87.
25. Ibid.
26. Ibid.; Targ and Katra, *Miracles of the Mind*, 142-143.
27. See, for example, Caryle Hirshberg and Marc Ian Barasch, *Remarkable Recovery: What Extraordinary Healings Tell Us About Getting Well and Staying Well* (New York: Riverhead Books, 1995); MacNutt, *Healing*; Gladys Taylor McGary with Jess Stearn, *The Physician Within You: Medicine for the New Millenium* (Deerfield Beach, FL: Health Communications, Inc., 1997); James Pruitt, *Healed by Prayer* (New York: Avon Books, 1999); Ron Roth with Peter Occhiogrosso, *Holy Spirit for Healing: Merging Ancient Wisdom with Modern Medicine* (Carlsbad, CA: Hay House, Inc., 2001); and Dan Wakefield, *Expect a Miracle: The Miraculous Things That Happen to Ordinary People* (New York: HarperCollins, 1995).
28. Randolph C. Byrd, "Positive therapeutic effects of intercessory prayer in a coronary care unit population," *Southern Medical Journal*, Vol. 81, No. 7, 1988, pp. 826-829.
29. The "p" value is the probability that the change measured in a study could be due to chance, here being at the 0.05 or 5 percent level.

Most researchers consider p values of 0.05 or less as indicating that a change was statistically significant. Therefore, a p value of 0.05 or 5 percent is at the limit for saying that a change was significant.

30. William S. Harris, Manohar Gowda, Jerry W. Kolb, and others, "A randomized, controlled trial of the effects of remote, intercessory prayer on outcomes in patients admitted to the coronary care unit," *Archives of Internal Medicine*, Vol. 159, No. 19, 1999, pp. 2273-2278.

31. Mitchell W. Krucoff, Suzanne W. Crater, Diane Gallup, and others. "Music, imagery, touch, and prayer as adjuncts to interventional cardiac care: the Monitoring and Actualisation of Noetic Trainings (MANTRA) II randomised study," *Lancet* 2005, Vol. 366, 2006, pp. 211-217.

32. See reviews of randomized studies of prayer and healing by John A. Astin, Elaine Harkness and Edzard Ernst, "The efficacy of 'distant healing': A systematic review of randomized trials," *Annals of Internal Medicine*, Vol. 132, No. 11, 2000, pp. 903-910 and by Mark Townsend, Virginia Kladder, Hana Ayele and Thomas Mulligan, "Systematic review of clinical trials examining the effects of religion on health," *Southern Medical Journal*, Vol. 95, No. 11, 2002, pp. 1429-1434.

33. Mt. 6:6. See also Barbara Fiand, *Prayer and the Quest for Healing: Our Personal Transformation and Cosmic Responsibility* (New York: The Crossroad Publishing Company, 1999), 7.

34. Bruce G. Epperly, *God's Touch: Faith, Wholeness, and the Healing Miracles of Jesus* (Louisville, KY: Westminster John Knox Press, 2001); Fiand, *Prayer and the Quest for Healing*, 7; MacNutt, *Healing*, 26; Norbert and Webber, *Stretch Out Your Hand*, 34; Roth with Ochiogrosso, *The Healing Path of Prayer*, 43.

35. Norberg and Webber, *Stretch Out Your Hand*, 58; Mark A. Pearson, *Christian Healing: A Practical and Comprehensive Guide, Second Edition* (Grand Rapids, MI: Chosen Books, 1995), 57-59; Catherine Ponder, *The Dynamic Laws of Healing* (Marina del Rey, CA: DeVorss & Company, 1985), 115; Roth with Ochiogrosso, *The Healing Path of Prayer*, 16-17, 21, 117, 122; Targ and Katra, *Miracles of the Mind*, 5, 143, 266.

36. Mk. 11:24. See also Mt. 7:7-8 and Jn. 16:23-24. See also Barbara Schlemon Ryan, *Healing Prayer: Spiritual Pathways to Health and Wellness* (Cincinnati, OH: St. Anthony Messenger Press, 2001), 47-49.

37. Harpur, *The Uncommon Touch*, 187; MacNutt, *Healing*, 103; Roth with Ochiogrosso, *The Healing Path of Prayer*, 45.

38. MacNutt, *Healing*, 157-166; Francis MacNutt, *The Power to Heal* (Notre Dame, IN: Ave Maria Press, 1977), 179.

39. MacNutt, *Healing*, 157-166. MacNutt (page 164) suggests that use of "your will" can weaken the effect of prayer because it expresses an element of doubt, in that we do not believe that "ordinarily it is God's will to heal persons who ask."

40. Ibid., 120-122.

41. Jn. 16:23.

42. Neil Douglas-Klotz, *Prayers of the Cosmos: Meditations on the Aramaic Words of Jesus* (San Francisco: HarperSanFrancisco, 1990), 86-88; Roth with Ochiogrosso, *The Healing Path of Prayer*, 72.

43. MacNutt, *Healing*, 99; Ryan, *Healing Prayer*, 32-33.

44. Douglas Connelly, *Angels Around Us: What the Bible Really Says* (Downers Grove, IL: InterVarsity Press, 1994), 16.

45. Maria Pia Giudici, *The Angels: Spiritual and Exegetical Notes*, translated from the Italian by Edmund C. Lane (New York: Alba House, 1993), 57.

46. "Are not all angels ministering spirits sent to serve those who will experience salvation?" (Heb. 1:14.)

47. Connelly, *Angels Around Us*, 22; Giudici, *The Angels*, 103-107; Flach, *Faith, Healing, and Miracles*, 47, 52.

48. MacNutt, *The Power to Heal*, 29; Ryan, *Healing Prayer*, 53.

49. Lk. 11:9; Mt. 7:7.

50. Lk. 11:5-8.

51. MacNutt, *The Power to Heal*, 32.

52. Harpur, *The Uncommon Touch*, 16; Linda L. Smith, *Called into Healing: Reclaiming Our Judeo-Christian Legacy of Healing Touch* (Arvada, CO: HTSM Press, 2000), 75.

53. Mk. 16:17-18.

54. Acts 9:36-41; 28:7-8.

55. James 5:14.

56. Donna Eden with David Feinstein, *Energy Medicine* (New York: Jeremy P. Tarcher/Putnam, 1998), 96-98; Richard Gerber, *Vibrational Medicine for the 21st Century: The Complete Guide to Energy Healing and Spiritual Transformation* (New York: Eagle Brook, 2000), 16-17.

57. Barbara Ann Brennan, *Hands of Light: A Guide to Healing Through the Human Energy Field* (New York: Bantam Books, 1987), 41-42, 48.

58. Ibid., 42-53; Gerber, *Vibrational Medicine for the 21st Century*, 47-73.

59. Brennan, *Hands of Light*, 43; Gerber, *Vibrational Medicine for the 21st Century,* 17-21.

60. Brennan, *Hands of Light*, 45-46.

61. Brennan, *Hands of Light*, 43; Smith, *Called into Healing,* 8-10.

62. Brennan, *Hands of Light*, 45; Gerber, *Vibrational Medicine for the 21st Century*, 20-21.

Part IV: A Healing Service

1. Carolyn Stahl Bohler, *Opening to God: Guided Imagery Meditation on Scripture* (Nashville, TN: Upper Room Books, 1996); Anthony De Mello, *Sadhana - A Way to God: Christian Exercises in the Eastern Form* (New York: Image Books Doubleday, 1978); Thich Nhat Hanh, *The Blooming of a Lotus: Guided Meditation for Achieving the Miracle of Mindfulness*, translated by Annabel Laity (Boston: Beacon Press, 1993); Stephen Levine, *Guided Meditations, Explorations and Healings* (New York: Anchor Books, 1991); Patty McCullough, *Touching Jesus: 20 Guided Meditations on His Care and Compassion* (Notre Dame, IN: Ave Maria Press, 2001); Bobby Ogden, *Experiencing God in His Word and World: Guided Meditations in the Psalms* (Belleville, Ontario, Canada: Guardian Books, 2004); Isaias Powers, *Heart-Talks with Jesus: Guided Scripture Meditations* (Mystic, CT: Twenty-Third Publications, 1998).
2. Reprinted with the permission of Elizabeth Roberts and Elias Amidon from: Elizabeth Roberts and Elias Amidon, editors, *Life Prayers from Around the World: 365 Prayers, Blessings, and Affirmations to Celebrate the Human Journey* (San Francisco: HarperSanFrancisco, 1996), 14; copyright © 1996 by Elizabeth Roberts and Elias Amidon.
3. Excerpted from: John Kirvan, *Let Nothing Disturb You: A Journey to the Center of the Soul With Teresa of Avila* (Notre Dame, IN; Ave Maria Press), 6; copyright © 1996 by Quest Associates.
4. Excerpted from: Maggie Oman, editor, *Prayers for Healing: 365 Blessings, Poems, and Meditations from Around the World* (Berkeley, CA: Conari Press, imprint of Red Wheel/Weiser, 1997), 206; copyright © 1997 by Maggie Oman. To order call 1-800-423-7087.
5. Reprinted with the permission of the Citadel Press from: Kahlil Gibran, *Secrets of the Heart: Meditations of Kahlil Gibran* (Kansas City, MO: Hallmark Cards, 1968), 19. This book was reprinted by arrangement with The Citadel Press from *A Treasury of Kahlil Gibran*, copyright © 1951 by The Citadel Press and from *A Second Treasury of Kahlil Gibran*, copyright © 1962 by The Citadel Press.
6. Reprinted with the permission of Jim Cohn from: Oman, *Prayers for Healing*, 90.
7. Reprinted with the permission of Barry Harris from: Barry Harris, *Something at the Center* (New York: iUniverse, 2003), 7; copyright © 2003 by Barry Harris.

8. Reprinted with the permission of Dawna Markova from: Oman, *Prayers for Healing*, 41. The website for Dawna Markova, Ph.D, is www.SmartWired.org.

9. Reprinted with the permission of the Office of Public Information, Bahá'í International Community, from: Oman, *Prayers for Healing*, 41.

10. Reprinted with the permission of Daniel Ladinsky from Daniel Ladinsky, translator, *The Gift: Poems by Hafiz* (New York: Penguin Compass, 1999), 270; copyright © 1999 by Daniel Ladinsky.

11. Verses 1 and 2 of "All People That on Earth Do Dwell." Words by William Kethe (1561) and music ("Old Hundredth") attributed to Louis Bourgeois (1551). The words and music are in the public domain.

12. Verse 1 of "Precious Lord, Take My Hand." The words and music are by Thomas A. Dorsey; © copyright 1938 by Unichapell Music Inc. Copyright renewed. International copyright secured. All rights reserved. The words are reprinted with the permission of Unichapell Music Inc.

13. Verses 1 and 3 of "O Holy Spirit, Root of Life." The words are by Jean Janzen, based on writings of Hildegard of Bingen (1098-1179); © copyright 1991 by Jean Janzen. The music is from the Trier Manuscript (1852), adapted by Michael Praetorius (1609). The music is in the public domain. The words are reprinted with the permission of Jean Janzen.

14. "Spirit of the Living God." Words and music by Daniel Iverson (1926). The words and music are in the public domain.

15. Verses 1 and 3 of "Breathe on Me, Breath of God." Words by Edwin Hatch (1878) and music by Robert Jackson (1888). The words and music are in the public domain.

16. Verses 1 and 3 of "For the Beauty of the Earth." Original words by Folliott S. Pierpoint (1864) and music by Conrad Kocher (1838). The words and music are in the public domain.

17. Verse 1 of "This Little Light of Mine." Words of an African-American spiritual and music © copyright by various composers and arrangers. The words are in the public domain.

18. Verses 1 and 3 of "Amazing Grace." Original words by John Newton (1779) and music of the early Protestant Hymn, "New Britain," which was subsequently arranged by Edwin O. Excell (1900). The words and music are in the public domain.

19. "Open My Eyes, That I May See." Words and music by Clara H. Scott (1895). The words and music are in the public domain.

20. Verses 1 and 3 of "Come Forth, O Love Divine." Words by Bianco da Siena (15th Century), translated to the original words in English by Richard F. Littledale (1867), and music © copyright 1906 by Ralph Vaughan Williams. The words are in the public domain.

21. Reprinted with the permission of the publisher, The Continuum International Publishing Group, from: Paul M. Allen and Joan deRis Allen, *Francis of Assisi's Canticle of the Creatures: A Modern Spiritual Path* (New York: Continuum, 1996), 134; copyright © 1996 by Paul M. Allen and Joan deRis Allen.

22. Reprinted with the permission of Elizabeth Roberts and Elias Amidon from: Roberts and Amidon, *Life Prayers from Around the World*, 298.

23. Excerpted from: Maggie Oman, editor, *Prayers for Healing*, 146.

24. Reprinted with the permission of the publisher, The Continuum International Publishing Group, from: Allen and Allen, *Francis of Assisi's Canticle of the Creatures*, 23-24.

25. Excerpted from: Maggie Oman, editor, *Prayers for Healing*, 38.

26. Ibid., 186-187. This prayer was reprinted from A Garland of Love by Daphne Rose Kingma, published by Conari Press, imprint of Red Wheel/Weiser; copyright © 1992 by Daphne Rose Kingma.

27. Reprinted with the permission of the Paulist Press from: J. Philip Newell, *Celtic Prayers from Iona* (Nahwah, NJ: Paulist Press, 1997), 27; copyright © 1997 by Dr. J. Philip Newell.

28. Reprinted with the permission of Linda L. Smith from: Linda L. Smith, *Called into Healing: Reclaiming Our Judeo-Christian Legacy of Healing Touch* (Arvada, CO: HTSM Press, 2000), 235; copyright © by Linda L. Smith.

29. Verse 1 of "God Be with You Till We Meet Again." Original words by Jeremiah E. Rankin (1880) and music by William G. Tomer (1880). The words and music are in the public domain.

30. Verse 1 of "God, Dismiss Us with Your Blessing (adapted)." Original words attributed to John Fawcett (1773) and music to an 18th Century Sicilian melody published in The European Magazine Review (1792). The words and music are in the public domain.

31. "God Be with You." Words and music by Thomas A. Dorsey and Artelia W. Hutchins (1940); © copyright 1940 by Unichapell Music Inc. Copyright renewed. International copyright secured. All rights reserved. The words are reprinted with the permission of Unichapell Music Inc.

32. "Blest Be the Tie That Binds." Words by John Fawcett (1872) and music by Johann G. Nägeli (1828) as arranged by Lowell Mason (1845). The words and music are in the public domain.

33. "Alleluia." The traditional eight-fold Alleluia. The music is copyright © by various composers.

Reading List

George Appleton, general editor, *The Oxford Book of Prayer* (New York: Oxford University Press, 1985).

Kenneth L. Bakken, *The Journey into God: Healing and the Christian Faith* (Minneapolis, MN: Augsburg Fortress, 2000).

Carolyn Stahl Bohler, *Opening to God: Guided Imagery Meditation on Scripture* (Nashville, TN: Upper Room Books, 1996).

Barbara Ann Brennan, *Hands of Light: A Guide to Healing Through the Human Energy Field* (New York: Bantam Books, 1987).

Ruth Cranston, *The Miracle of Lourdes: Updated and Expanded Edition by the Medical Bureau of Lourdes* (New York: Image Books, 1988).

Stevan L. Davies, *Jesus the Healer: Possession, Trance, and the Origin of Christianity* (New York: Continuum, 1995).

Anthony De Mello, *Sadhana - A Way to God: Christian Exercises in the Eastern Form* (New York: Image Books, 1978).

Larry Dossey, *Reinventing Medicine: Beyond Mind-Body to a New Era of Healing* (San Francisco: HarperSanFrancisco, 1999).

Thomas A. Droege, *The Faith Factor in Healing* (Philadelphia: Trinity Press International, 1991).

Bruce G. Epperly, *God's Touch: Faith, Wholeness, and the Healing Miracles of Jesus* (Louisville, KY: Westminster John Knox Press, 2001).

Barbara Fiand, *Prayer and the Quest for Healing: Our Personal Transformation and Cosmic Responsibility* (New York: Crossroad Publishing, 1999).

Frederic Flach, *Faith, Healing, and Miracles* (New York: Hatherleigh Press, 2000).

Tom Harpur, *The Uncommon Touch: An Investigation of Spiritual Healing* (Toronto, Ontario: McClelland & Stewart Inc., 1994).

Caryle Hirshberg and Marc Ian Barasch, *Remarkable Recovery: What Extraordinary Healings Tell Us About Getting Well and Staying Well* (New York: Riverhead Books, 1995).

Morton Kelsey, *Healing and Christianity: A Classic Study* (Minneapolis, MN: Augsburg Fortress, 1995).

Howard Clark Key, *Medicine, Miracle and Magic in New Testament Times* (New York: Cambridge University Press, 1986).

Harold G. Koenig, *Is Religion Good for Your Health? The Effects of Religion on Physical and Mental Health* (New York: Haworth Pastoral Press, 1997).

Francis MacNutt, *The Power to Heal* (Notre Dame, IN: Ave Maria Press, 1977).

Francis MacNutt, *Healing* (Notre Dame, IN: Ave Maria Press, 1999).

Tilda Norberg and Robert D. Webber, *Stretch Out Your Hand: Exploring Healing Prayer* (Nashville, TN: Upper Room Books, 1998).

Maggie Oman, editor, *Prayers for Healing: 365 Blessings, Poems, and Meditations from Around the World* (Berkeley, CA: Conari Press, 1997).

Elizabeth Roberts and Elias Amidon, editors, *Life Prayers from Around the World: 365 Prayers, Blessings, and Affirmations to Celebrate the Human Journey* (San Francisco: HarperSanFrancisco, 1996).

Ron Roth with Peter Occhiogrosso, *The Healing Path of Prayer: A Modern Mystic's Guide to Spiritual Power* (New York: Three Rivers Press, 1997).

Ron Roth with Peter Occhiogrosso, *Holy Spirit for Healing: Merging Ancient Wisdom with Modern Medicine* (Carlsbad, CA: Hay House, Inc., 2001).

Russell Targ and Jane Katra, *Miracles of the Mind: Exploring Nonlocal Consciousness and Spiritual Healing* (Novato, CA: New World Library, 1999).